Yew & Non-Yew

*'I do not presume
to condemn all
mixed planting,
only stupid and ignorant
mixed planting'*
Gertrude Jekyll

Published by Century Books in 1996

1 3 5 7 9 10 8 6 4 2

First published in the United Kingdom by Century 1996

Century Books Limited
20 Vauxhall Bridge Road, London, SW1V 2SA

Random House Australia (Pty) Limited
16 Dalmore Drive, Scoresby, Victoria, 3179

Random House New Zealand Limited
18 Poland Road, Glenfield
Auckland 10, New Zealand

Random House South Africa (Pty) Limited
PO Box 2263, Rosebank 2121, South Africa
Random House UK Limited Reg. No. 954009

A CIP catalogue record for this book
is available from the British Library

Papers used by Random House UK Limited
are natural, recyclable products made from wood grown in
sustainable forests. The manufacturing processes conform to
the environmental regulations of the country of origin

ISBN 0 07 1267705 4

Designed by Jerry Goldie Graphic Design
Origination by R&B Creative Services
Printed and bound in Great Britain by
Mackays of Chatham plc

Yew & Non-Yew

Gardening for Horticultural Climbers

JAMES BARTHOLOMEW

CENTURY

To Anne and Beatrice

OH NO! NOT PRIVET!

One Monday, the editor of a certain national newspaper was in relaxed and friendly mood. He found time to make small-talk with one of his underlings - me. He asked if I had enjoyed a good weekend. I told him the most interesting thing I could remember about it: that I had planted a hedge.

Being a keen gardener, he suddenly took a new interest. His eyes descended from the ceiling where they had been wandering about and he inquired, focussing sharply on me,

'What sort of hedge?'

'Privet,' I replied

His expression changed.

'Privet?' he repeated, looking surprised.

I nodded.

'Privet!' he said again, surprise turning into horror. 'Oh no! Surely not privet!'

He kept repeating, as people do when they are in shock, 'Oh no! Not privet!'

He put his hand to his head - appalled. In all his experience of the world in a lifetime of journalism - covering wars, corruption and even party conferences - he had clearly never come across anything quite as shocking.

He proceeded to tell me - with an emphasis that only employees of his newspaper (and their widows) can imagine - that I should not have planted privet.

I should have planted yew.

CONTENTS

CHAPTER ONE

YEW AND NON-YEW GARDENS

P lants do not inherently belong to the class system. But where nature has failed to make social distinctions, the British have stepped in to put the matter right. The garden has become one of the last bright sparks among the dying embers of British class.

The landed gentry may have been dispossessed. The regiments of the officer class may have been disbanded. Even vicars are not what they used to be. But, impoverished and disheartened, the upper classes still set themselves apart – through their gardens.

There may not be 'Two Nations' any more but there are two nations of gardeners. They garden in completely different ways, with different plants arranged to make different effects. They even use different kinds of garden paving and furniture.

Most television programmes and books pretend this division of the horticultural classes does not exist. But when a presenter of 'Gardener's World' on BBC television, holds up the latest hybrid petunia and says how wonderful it is, half of the audience is delighted and the other half is groaning with a bout of nausea.

The socially superior garden is a state of mind as much as an arrangement of vegetation. At its root is the British upper-class person's wish to imagine himself a nineteenth- or eighteenth-century squire – or at least a 'gentleman' – regardless of the fact that these days he is, unfortunately, an advertising executive, banker or pop singer. The garden must fit his self-image. It must 'go' with his old house (which similarly has been bought to confirm his delightful fantasy).

The patron saint of this sort of gardening is Gertrude Jekyll who was the first to create the modern, upmarket mixture of formal paths combined with informal planting. She was part of the Arts and Crafts movement which helped to convince the upper classes that they should loathe man-made materials such as plastic – sticking, instead, with old-fashioned wood or stone (however inconvenient, expensive and heavy this might be).

This sort of garden is restrained and well-behaved. The plants are discreet. They flower occasionally but never would they dream of being 'vulgar' or 'garish'. The plants cherished most ardently

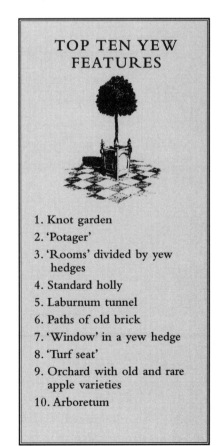

TOP TEN YEW FEATURES

1. Knot garden
2. 'Potager'
3. 'Rooms' divided by yew hedges
4. Standard holly
5. Laburnum tunnel
6. Paths of old brick
7. 'Window' in a yew hedge
8. 'Turf seat'
9. Orchard with old and rare apple varieties
10. Arboretum

– such as evergreen viburnums, euphorbias and hellebores – are those which barely flower at all.

Species plants and plants bred before the end of the nineteenth century are particularly liked (especially roses named after French ladies). Stoically, the upmarket gardener endures the fact that these earlier plants tend to flower only once a year and for a relatively short time. Heroically he does not complain that they are also more prone to disease and other problems.

Formal hedging is often a feature. Yew (or perhaps beech) is used for the high hedges (sometimes planted to create 'rooms' – in imitation of the famous gardens at Hidcote and Sissinghurst). Box is used for low hedges at the edges of the flower beds. The paths are made of natural materials such as York stone or pea shingle. The benches are made of hardwood (hard by name and hard by nature).

All this is a world away from the other kind of commonly seen garden. This kind is unpretentious, practical and cheerful. The paved area near the house is as big as possible – much more convenient for barbecues from which the smoke of burning paraffin wafts across to the lucky people next door.

The paving is made of concrete. This is relatively cheap and can be cast to look 'just like real stone'. Hanging baskets drip from the porch or the wall – luxuriating in colour combinations that would frighten a rainbow.

This gardener goes in for annuals – petunias, busy lizzies, lobelias – with the enthusiasm of a Victorian park administrator. The more violent colours he can squeeze in, the better. His perennials are colour-blasters: chrysanthemums, dahlias and gladioli.

The best blooms, quite obviously, must be the biggest

The really advanced gardener of this type goes in for competitions to make huge blooms. He might grow 'football chrysanthemums' – so named as testament to their startling size and in honour of his favourite game. Alternatively he might go in for vegetables: giant carrots or obscenely enormous cucumbers.

His style reflects a different idea of what a garden is for. His basic assumption is that a garden is about flowers. Flowers, he believes, are meant to be colourful. He concludes that the ideal garden must be one with with the most flowers and – quite logically as it seems to him – the brightest colours. The best blooms, quite obviously, must be the biggest.

He also expects the garden to be a place of entertainment for himself and his friends – hence the bright blue swimming pool immediately next to the patio. A team of white plastic chairs with comfortable cushions is ready and waiting for a sunny day.

Thank heavens that this gardener has a sense of humour. Or is it such a blessing? He is the chap at the garden centre buying that concrete figure of a smiling frog rowing a boat. Or he might be buying the miniature fountain featuring a blue, polystyrene, naked lady. He is bound to be tempted by the kidney-shaped pond into which water flows with the delicate sound of a loo cistern filling up.

So – two nations of gardeners and two utterly different styles. A horticultural gulf that separates the country. A phrase to sum it up is not hard to find. Britain's social divide was once examined in a book

TOP TEN NON-YEW FEATURES

1. Concrete frog in rowing boat
2. Blue, naked lady, ready-made fountain
3. White plastic Grecian urns
4. Hanging baskets which descend for watering
5. Kidney-shaped pre-fabricated pond
6. Flower pots which attach themselves to drainpipes
7. Mixed colour, concrete paving stones
8. Rotary laundry line
9. Built-in barbecue
10. Green plastic dog 'loo'

QUESTIONNAIRE – ARE YOU AN UPMARKET GARDENER?

Answer these questions and find out:

(if no answer is exactly right, tick the closest)

1. What kind of hedge do you have most of?

a) Yew, beech, holly and/or box ☐

b) Privet, leylandii or any other conifer ☐

2. Is the patio made of

a) concrete ☐

b) concrete cast to resemble stone ☐

c) concrete slabs of varied colours ☐

d) re-constituted stone ☐

e) York stone ☐

f) old bricks ☐

3. Which of these plants do you have in your garden?

a) alliums ☐

b) gladioli ☐

c) euphorbias ☐

d) hellebores ☐

e) snapdragons ☐

f) mixed colour petunias ☐

g) ivy with the word 'gold' in the name. ☐

4. If you have roses in your garden are they predominantly:

a) modern ones (floribundas or hybrid teas) ☐

b) 'patio' ☐

c) old roses named after French ladies ☐

d) species or shrub roses ☐

e) you do not have roses at all ☐

5. What are your garden sculptures made of?

a) Bronze or stone ☐

b) re-constituted stone (as per Haddonstone, Chilstone or similar) ☐

c) plastic, polystyrene or concrete ☐

d) you have no sculptures ☐

6. Is the arch/arbour/pergola in your garden made of

a) metal coated in plastic ☐

b) prefabricated wood ☐

c) iron or custom-made wood ☐

d) brick ☐

e) stone ☐

f) you do not have one ☐

7. Is your pond made waterproof by

a) prefabricated polystyrene ☐

b) Polythene ☐

c) concrete ☐

d) puddled clay ☐

e) it is a natural pond ☐

f) you don't have one ☐

8. How many of the following do you have in your garden

a) Plastic Grecian urn ☐

b) hanging basket ☐

c) gnome ☐

d) plastic heron ☐

edited by Nancy Mitford called *Noblesse Oblige*. One of the essays, by Alan Ross, used the phrase 'U and Non-U' to distinguish upper-class language from the rest. The phrase passed into the language to define upper-class and non-upper-class behaviour. Given the kind of hedge which upmarket gardeners strongly prefer, the horticultural equivalent of this phrase seems delightfully obvious: Yew and Non-Yew.

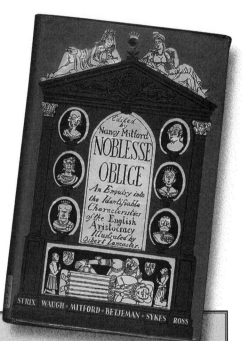

HOW TO SCORE:

1. a) 3 points, b) zero.

2. a) zero, b) minus one, c) minus two, d) 1, e) 3, f) 5.

3. score 1 point each for a), c), d). Score minus one each for the rest.

4. a) zero, b) minus 1, c) 3, d) 4, e) 2.

5. a) 4, b) 1, c) minus 3, d) 1.

6. a) minus 2, b) 2, c) 4, d) 5, e) 6, f) 2.

7. a) minus 3, b) 1, c) 2, d) 4, e) 5, f) 1.

8. minus 2 for each tick.

HOW YOU RATE:

15 to 30 points: You are an unbearable gardening snob.

5 to 15 points: You are a 'Yew' gardener of distinction without being a bore about it.

Minus 5 to plus 5 points: You are borderline. You might be a Non-Yew gardener who has been reading books by Rosemary Verey and has become confused. Alternatively you could be an upper-class type who puts convenience dangerously high on your list of priorities.

Minus 5 to minus 15 points: You are certifiably 'Non-Yew'. You are so unpretentious that people remark upon it. What a riot of wonderful colour your garden must be.

Minus 15 to minus 23: You are Alan Titchmarsh.

CHAPTER TWO

HOW TO BE A HAUGHTY-CULTURALIST

Apparently certain people are likely to read this book not, as they should, as a serious sociological analysis but as a handy guide to snobbish gardening. I am appalled. However one needs all the readers one can get. So here it is:

The first thing to do is to remove all traces of Non-Yewness. Every object in the garden made of plastic or concrete must go. The charming little model of a fantasy castle must be smashed. The gnomes must be deported.

The concrete paving must go on to the skip. Anything made into the shape of a kidney must be removed. The hanging baskets must be dropped.

You might plead that the free-standing barbecue is terrifically practical. Too bad. That must go, too. It makes the owner look more like a double-glazing salesman than a Yew gardener.

The Pampas Grass can go back to the pampas where it belongs. The Leylandii hedge must be uprooted and transported away – if you can get a big enough lorry. You must renounce the tomato gro-bag and clean out the rotary laundry-line. This is meant to be a display of plants, not underwear.

You must give up any attempts you may have made in the past to grow the biggest potato or cucumber or anything else in the competition run by your local horticultural society. As a Yew gardener, you are meant to rise above such vulgarity. The competition on which you have now embarked is much more subtle.

Into the bin go your Bakker and Mr Fothergill's catalogues with their dazzling colours. You can keep the Thompson and Morgan catalogue but only if you avert your eyes from the mixed-colour offerings.

The next step is to educate yourself. Subscribe to the 'right' sort of gardening magazines. Cancel your subscription to *Garden Answers* and take out subscriptions to *Hortus*, *Gardens Illustrated*, *Garden Design* and perhaps even *Pacific Horticulture*.

You do not need to do everything that *Hortus* approves. That would be taking snobbery too far.

TOP GARDENING MAGAZINES AND COLUMNS

Yew

1. *Pacific Horticulture* (American)
2. *Hortus*
3. *Gardens Illustrated*
4. *Garden Design* (American)
5. *World of Interiors* (when doing exteriors)
6. *The Garden* (journal of the Royal Horticultural Society)
7. *Perspectives* (when doing gardens)
8. *Financial Times* (Robin Lane-Fox)
9. *The Independent* (Anna Pavord)
10. *Architectural Digest* (when doing gardens – American)

Non-Yew

1. *Garden News.*
2. *Amateur Gardening.*
3. *Your Garden.*
4. *Garden Answers.*
5. *Gardener's World.*

But *Hortus* does at least give an idea of how far garden snobbery can be taken.

You really score with *Garden Design*. It is American and therefore your friends are unlikely to have it. It will put you one ahead of the Jekylls or Sackville-Wests next door. It also happens to be better than most British gardening magazines. The text is a bit gushy (well, it is American) but the use of photographs is superb.

Pacific Horticulture is best of all. It is foreign and learned and, what is more, Rosemary Verey knows the editor. But it is better for leaving casually on coffee

LECTURES AND COURSES

A pleasurable part of becoming a Yew gardener is going to lectures and making garden visits. *Gardens Illustrated* lists a selection of these every month. But the aspiring Yew gardener will naturally want to concentrate on the most select and upmarket.

VISITS TO GARDENS:

The visits you want are those to gardens which are not generally open to the public. This means that when you talk about your visits you leave the impression that you are welcome in the best private gardens across the world. There are many companies organising trips nowadays – some of them are even mainstream travel agents. The specialist one to go for is Border Lines in West Sussex. Another that is perfectly acceptable is Green Fingers. Others will do, provided they have bought the services of one of the top garden gurus.

LECTURES:

The most Yew place for a garden lecture is Christie's. There – as you listen to an obscure talk by an academic – you might find yourself in the same row as Jacob Rothschild who is fabulously rich, bears a title and has wonderful taste. He is such a serious aesthete that he spent six years looking for someone suitable to design the area around his swimming pool in Corfu. The lecture which you and he are attending could well be barely audible and crushingly boring but never mind. You were there. Other Yew places to be lectured are The English Gardening School at Chelsea Physic Garden, the Garden History Society and the Museum of Garden History.

SHORT COURSES:

It is as well to build up a smattering of horticultural knowledge. The place to go is tables than using as a guide. The best magazine for that is *Gardens Illustrated*.

You had better buy some books. For a full listing of Yew books see chapter 9. But for a crash course, concentrate on a few. Rosemary Verey's *Making of a Garden* shows the kind of effect you should be trying to imitate. Rosemary Verey is very Yew. If she says something is all right, it is.

Another accessible book to go for would be Roy Strong's *Small Traditional Gardens*. This has some garden plans. Strong will help you introduce the necessary element of formality into your garden.

Obviously you must join the Royal Horticultural Society if you have not already done so. You should also join the Garden History Society which has lectures on just the sorts of things you ought to know about such as the Renaissance gardens of France and Italy. Another organisation you should join if you want to keep on growing vegetables is the Henry Doubleday Research Association. This supplies historic vegetable seeds which are superior, in several senses, to the seeds you get from an ordinary catalogue.

Your education as a gardener should be completed by visits to the great gardens of Europe such as Het Loo and Isola Bella. If you can't run to that, you had better make do with some of the Yew gardens of Britain such as Hidcote Manor, Sissinghurst and the newly restored Privy Garden at Hampton Court.

The next job is to concentrate on getting

the English Gardening School. Those present will mostly be ladies. They can be divided into three types: 1. Ladies who want to become professional gardeners (sort of), 2. Ladies who have married big gardens, and 3. Ladies who lunch. No combination could be more Yew. The first type confers credibility, the second social status and the third what passes in Britain for style.

LONG COURSES:
Don't bother. They would tell you far more than you need to know about botany and so on. If you insist, go to the Inchbald for a fearfully intensive course lasting three terms. This will enable you to bore for Britain. It will not, however, get you any closer to haughty-culture.

ANNUAL CALENDAR
FOR THE YEW GARDENER

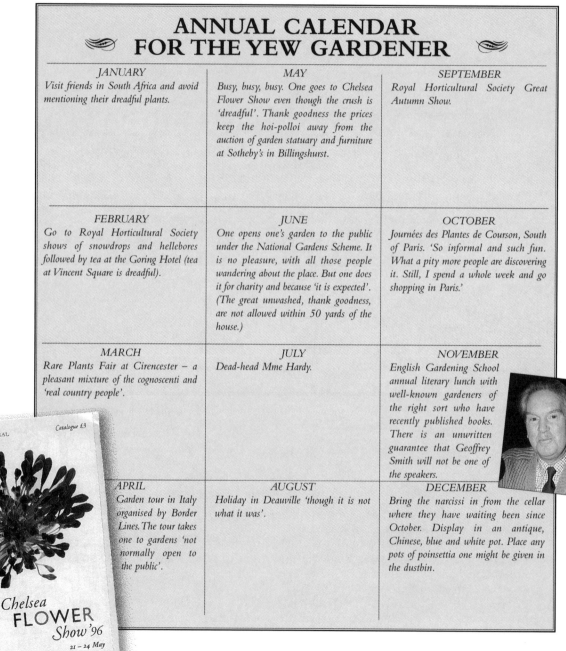

JANUARY
Visit friends in South Africa and avoid mentioning their dreadful plants.

MAY
Busy, busy, busy. One goes to Chelsea Flower Show even though the crush is 'dreadful'. Thank goodness the prices keep the hoi-polloi away from the auction of garden statuary and furniture at Sotheby's in Billingshurst.

SEPTEMBER
Royal Horticultural Society Great Autumn Show.

FEBRUARY
Go to Royal Horticultural Society shows of snowdrops and hellebores followed by tea at the Goring Hotel (tea at Vincent Square is dreadful).

JUNE
One opens one's garden to the public under the National Gardens Scheme. It is no pleasure, with all those people wandering about the place. But one does it for charity and because 'it is expected'. (The great unwashed, thank goodness, are not allowed within 50 yards of the house.)

OCTOBER
Journées des Plantes de Courson, South of Paris. 'So informal and such fun. What a pity more people are discovering it. Still, I spend a whole week and go shopping in Paris.'

MARCH
Rare Plants Fair at Cirencester – a pleasant mixture of the cognoscenti and 'real country people'.

JULY
Dead-head Mme Hardy.

NOVEMBER
English Gardening School annual literary lunch with well-known gardeners of the right sort who have recently published books. There is an unwritten guarantee that Geoffrey Smith will not be one of the speakers.

APRIL
Garden tour in Italy organised by Border Lines. The tour takes one to gardens 'not normally open to the public'.

AUGUST
Holiday in Deauville 'though it is not what it was'.

DECEMBER
Bring the narcissi in from the cellar where they have waiting been since October. Display in an antique, Chinese, blue and white pot. Place any pots of poinsettia one might be given in the dustbin.

L
TURAL

Catalogue £3

Chelsea
FLOWER
Show'96
21 – 24 May

you to think and talk like a Yew gardener. Two of the Gertrude Jekyll books *Home and Garden* and *Wood and Garden* should get you thinking as you ought. Miss Jekyll is gloriously politically incorrect.

You should also dip into a few other seminal works such as Russell Page's *Education of a Gardener*. No, you do not have to read the whole thing. You just need to get a flavour so that you can airily refer to such books in conversation. 'I think that Russell Page is just *too* austere. I suppose that is why so few of his gardens have survived,' you might say.

A few dips into Miles Hadfield's *A History of British Gardening* will enable you to say something like, 'Those early days of plant-hunting must have been very exciting. I was reading the other day about when Edward Wilson was imprisoned in Laokai for weeks, suspected of being a spy.'

If you can't run to the Villa d'Este, Hidcote Manor will do.

International references have a special quality. They show you are not merely upmarket, but upmarket on a global scale. You might try a comment like this, 'I think the American designer Olmsted was so right about using dark plants to bring out a distant view'.

Naturally you must go to Chelsea Flower Show every year to be aware of the current fashions and 'to have been'. If you cannot think of any other way to let people know, then you will be on safe ground if you complain about the crowds.

Lastly, let us not forget the business of actually making your Yew garden. Don't be too subtle. If you make a border in the style of Gertrude Jekyll, it could easily go unnoticed. Realistically, you cannot mark it with a label saying 'Gertrude Jekyll border'.

So go for a more emphatic statement. Make a knot garden. It is undeniably, aggressively Yew. It can have zero flowers and therefore no possible risk of vulgarity. It can be made of that Yew plant, box. And it carries with it whole centuries of upper-class gardening. In fact, when you are asked about the garden, it will be best if you can say, 'Oh yes, it is based on a design for a knot garden made in Holland in the seventeenth century'.

'Oh yes, it is based on a design for a knot garden made in Holland in the seventeenth century.'

As for the rest of the garden, surround it and divide it with non-stop yew hedges. The paths should be made of York stone, old bricks or, to save money, gravel. Buy some antique

THINGS THAT YEW GARDENERS SAY

'Of course, these are not really flowers at all, they are bracts.'

'I would not call it a garden at all. It is more like a gravel pit with a few weeds dotted about.'

(Probably about John Brookes' garden in Sussex)

'Yew is really much faster growing that most people think.'

'He is a very good plantsman, of course, but the garden is dreadfully *suburban.'*

'Such a pity about the modern plants.'

(To be said about practically any historical garden).

'I am going to have my trompe l'oeil *redone this summer.'*

'Gardener's Question Time is not what it was.'

'I always think of yew as the "little black dress" of the garden'

garden ornaments at auction from Sotheby's or Christie's. Make a few deep borders with shrubs and perennials which have been used by Jekyll and Verey or, for quick reference, use the relevant chapter in this book. Your new suppliers will include Green Farm Plants, Highfield Hollies and the Washfield Nursery.

Frankly this new garden will look pretty rough for the first five or seven years. Yew is notoriously slow-growing. That is why it is particularly important that you learn to talk about it well in the meantime. And you can keep your spirits up by going round to the Non-Yew gardens of your neighbours and being ostentatiously polite.

RESTORATION

A copper-bottomed guarantee of gardening superiority can be had for the price of a house in Surrey. It must, however, be one with a garden designed by Gertrude Jekyll.

Once you buy it, you must restore the garden with agonising accuracy. You must apply to the Reef Point Collection in California – where most Jekylliana is held – for the original planting plans. These you must follow as if obeying religious injunctions. If any plants in your garden have survived from the Jekyll era, you must save them and take cuttings so that they can be replaced, when they die, with exactly the same variety and strain.

The work, expense and the strait-jacketing of your own creativity will all bring their rewards. Visitors from all over the globe will purr with pleasure to be in a garden designed by the most renowned of modern gardeners. The county council will admire your project and might even support it with cash. The great and good will visit to chat and applaud.

Gardens by Jekyll are certain to be well regarded. But restoration can take other forms.

In Gloucestershire, a 'rococo' garden is being re-created at Painswick. A high Victorian garden has been brought back to colourful life in Regent's Park. There are many other projects under way or planned.

In Holland, the most celebrated restored garden is Het Loo which was laid out for William and Mary between 1686 and 1695. It has now become one of the 'must-see' gardens of the world.

One word of caution, though. Restoration is full of pitfalls. The surge of interest in historic and restored gardens has made gardeners far more critical than before. Yew gardeners have become like suspicious antique dealers, ever on the look-out for planting which is 'wrong' (that is, of the wrong period). Versailles, for example, has flower beds which are far more violent in colour and dense in planting than anything Louis XIV would have dreamt of. The new varieties in those beds simply did not exist in his day.

The enjoyable disgust, which the Yew gardener often feels when viewing historic gardens abroad, tends to confirm his suspicion that French and Italian culture is far too valuable to be left in the hands of the French and the Italians. In an ideal world, the cultural heritage of these two nations would be put under the control of the National Trust.

If you embark on a restoration of your own, you must expect the same high demands to be made of you. The last thing you want is to be accused of that most dreadful of all crimes against good taste: 'pastiche'.

Paul Getty – who thought he had led a tolerably successful life – now finds (after his death) that in fact he made a complete hash of it. The garden he created in America was based on Roman designs. It is – so they say – a 'pastiche'. Worse still, some have even been harsh enough to suggest that it is a 'Walt-Disney-style pastiche'. A reputation cannot easily recover from a blow like that.

However, one can take elements from historic gardens and plop them down where they seem appropriate. Rosemary Verey's knot garden is taken from Seventeenth-century books by Gervase Markham and Stephen Blake. Mrs Verey says, 'there is nothing wrong with copying. You will do it in your own way.'

If Rosemary Verey says it is all right, it is.

WHAT GARDENERS SAY...

YEW GARDENERS

'How colourful.'
TRANSLATION: How garish.

'How interesting.'
TRANSLATION: How awful.

'That Rosa 'Bobby Charlton' is doing very well.'
TRANSLATION: How embarrassing. I am in a garden which has hybrid tea roses.

'He's a wonderful plantsman.'
TRANSLATION: He's a terrible designer.

'These Agriframes pergolas are so practical.'
TRANSLATION: What vulgarity.

'You don't see chrysanthemums very often these days.'
TRANSLATION: I can see why.

'What an immaculate lawn!'
TRANSLATION: What a waste of time.

'Do you have trouble controlling that Leylandii hedge?'
TRANSLATION: Are you mad?

'......' (on seeing concrete block screening)
TRANSLATION: It makes you want to turn your face to the wall and die.

...AND WHAT THEY REALLY MEAN

NON-YEW GARDENERS

'That old rose variety gives a wonderful display.'
TRANSLATION:: After one good week, this garden will be over.

'This low hedge design is very interesting.'
TRANSLATION: Where are the flowers?

(About a knot garden) 'How often do you clip it?'
TRANSLATION: What is it *for*?

(of a restored William and Mary garden) 'This sparse planting is unusual.'
TRANSLATION: I suppose it is all right if you like looking at bare earth.

'With all these shrubs. I don't suppose you need to grow much from seed.'
TRANSLATION: You are not really a gardener at all.

'Do you ever eat out of doors?'
TRANSLATION: Where is the barbecue?

(Of paving) 'Nice York stone.'
TRANSLATION: More money than sense.

'Did that old statue come with the house, then?'
TRANSLATION: It needs a good clean.

(Of an antique stone bench) 'Do you use it much?'
TRANSLATION: Perfectly useless.

'That's a good-looking marrow.'
TRANSLATION: Mine is bigger than yours.

CHAPTER THREE

YEW AND NON-YEW PLANTS

Determining which plants are Yew is easy. All one has to do is look through the latest books by Rosemary Verey and Penelope Hobhouse to see which plants appear prominently in both. Any such plant must be absolutely 100 per cent, copper-bottomed Yew.

This approach reveals that the most Yew plant of all is currently euphorbia. Verey and Hobhouse both use euphorbia as though they had shares in them. Penelope Hobhouse appears on the back cover of her book *On Gardening* actually carrying a bunch of them. They both use a wide range of these somewhat poisonous creatures. The classic one is perhaps *Euphorbia characias ssp wulfenii* 'John Tomlinson'. The horrendously long name is reassuring. It should deter the great unwashed from buying it.

The great thing about euphorbias is that they don't really flower — at

Euphorbia

least not so that a non-gardener would notice. This is ideal for Yew gardeners. The danger of a flower colour clash is drastically reduced if one does not really have flowers at all. Even better, the euphorbia is a bold plant. It rises up and produces great clumps of these almost-flowers.

Euphorbia makes Yew gardeners feel they are being bold but tasteful. That is exactly what they want. It is the ideal sensation they long to experience. They want to feel they are bravely smashing conventions and restraints. But at the same time they want to do everything with elegance.

'Each year I get more enthusiastic about alliums.'

Penelope Hobhouse

Euphorbias are the answer. They make Yew gardeners feel ferocious yet graceful – a mixture of Attila the Hun and Margot Fonteyn.

Alliums fulfil a similar urge. Alliums are onions. They used to be confined to the kitchen garden. So how daring it is to bring them into the flower garden. What boldness! What a free spirit the gardener must be! And yet, at the same time, alliums are perfectly well behaved. 'Each year,' says Penelope Hobhouse, 'I get more enthusiastic about alliums.' Of course she does.

It is true they do produce balls of colour – generally a 'bad thing'. But these colours are so restrained or dark that they cause no offence. They tend to be somewhere between purple and blue. Rosemary has parallel rows of purple *Allium* alongside her laburnum walk. But this is a huge genus. The enthusiastic Yew gardener can explore it at length – finding onions that no one has ever heard of, let alone planted in their gardens. This is another aspect of plant choice for the advanced Yew gardener. One likes to have something rare.

The ideal plant for these enthusiasts is one that has only recently been discovered and which none of their friends yet possesses. It has been found on a recent plant-hunting expedition and is only available from a select nursery such as Green Farm Plants.

In the search for subtlety and understatement there is nothing to beat the hellebore. One of Penelope Hobhouse's books has a section headed 'A passion for hellebores'. This 'passion' would be practically incomprehensible to the Non-Yew gardener. The colours of hellebores are so subtle that you must be only about a foot away to see the colour at all. The flowers of *Helleborus × sternii* are a gentle green with an ultra-soft blush of reddish-purple. The flowers of *Helleborus foetidus* are just gentle green. That is it. There isn't even a blush of anything else.

As if this were not restrained enough, the flowers of most hellebores hang down and face the earth beneath them. So – to get a good look – you need to lie on the ground as well as being only a foot away.

There is, however, one hellebore over which hangs the shadow of disapproval from on high. Penelope Hobhouse hands out the black spot to *Helleborus niger* – the most common hellebore of all, often known as the Christmas rose. She remarks in true Yew style, 'I do not want large white flowers, much preferring the grace and subtle interest of the green hellebores.'

In the search for understatement, there is nothing to beat the hellebore

After all this, some people might be wondering whether any colour worthy of the name gets into a Yew garden. It does. But only in the most carefully selected ways.

Large individual flowers of strong colour are allowed provided that the colour is dark. The clematis 'Jackmanii superba' is perfectly acceptable because it keeps to its single colour and that colour is dark purple.

Strong colours can also sneak in because they are broken up among many small flowers. Verbenas are permissible because the heads of the flowers are broken up into scores of tiny florets. The same is true of wisterias and laburnums. The strong pinks and reds of pulmonarias are permitted because each flower is relatively small. Hardy geraniums are allowed in on the same basis. Kindly note that these geraniums are not the common bedding-out geraniums (strictly speaking 'pelargoniums') which are a different matter altogether.

There are three flowers – and probably not many more – which are allowed in the Yew garden despite the fact that they are both large and have strong, bright colours. In each case there is an excuse or explanation.

Bright yellow daffodils are allowed. They are acceptable because they are traditional and because early in the year there is a desperate shortage of colour in the garden. But they must be the right sort of daffodils. They must be simple, all-yellow daffodils. The johnny-come-lately hybrids with colour

They must be the right sort of daffodils

combinations such as a pink or orange trumpets coming out of white backgrounds are utterly forbidden. Nor must the flowers be 'double'. They must be simple and pure.

The second permissible plant that makes a blob of bright colour is the rose. It must, of course, be the right rose. This is a subject of such subtlety and importance that it has its own special section.

The third permissible large flower of bright colour is the tulip. It must, of course, be the right tulip, it must be in the right place and, what is more, it must be used in the right way. Yew gardeners are on dangerous ground with

FASHIONABLE PLANTS

Some plants are neither Yew nor Non-Yew. They are fashionable. Not many people actually use them, but they appear on television or in newspaper articles. In due course, some of them might become part of the mainstream but for the time being they are for those who are trying to be different.

Unfortunately, being different is quite difficult when gardening has been going on for thousands of years. The modern answer – as in modern art – has been to find plants which look repulsive, or at least aggressive. Hence the first prize for fashionability goes to *Cynara cardunculus* which is basically a very big thistle. It is an ugly spikey brute with attitude. A punk plant. Similarly aggressive are *Onopordum acanthium* and, in a wider variety of ways, the eryngiums. If you want your garden to look overgrown (verging on the hostile) this is the way to go.

The look was made particularly fashionable by Derek Jarman, the late film director. While he was dying of AIDS, he made a garden on the sea shore which featured tough, spikey plants that could tolerate the harsh conditions. The garden became very famous because his record of creating it has been a best-seller.

A similar strand in fashionable planting is the use of 'architectural plants' – plants that have a definite shape and can be used as specimen plants. Many of these architectural plants have sword-shaped leaves. They are not bought for their flowers though some of them are kind enough to flower occasionally. They are bought for their swords, which fall about them in a more or less regular way. Popular among these are ophiopogons, miscanthuses and phormiums. (The ophiopogon has a particular *cachet*, being so difficult to say.)

The first prize for fashionability goes to Cynara cardunculus which is basically an ugly spikey brute with attitude.

Quite different are the plants used in 'wild' or meadow gardens. The brilliant designer Dan Pearson uses a range of grasses and annuals which seed themselves. Unfortunately the style does not go well with the formal old houses that rich people tend to own. They admire the bravery and excitement of it all and then go back to their standard hollies.

Three individual plants to finish: *Gunnera manicata* is positively ugly and therefore terribly fashionable. It has vast leaves, bigger than umbrellas – a plant for scaring children. Ornamental cabbages are – or, rather, used to be – new and different. But they are loud and very recognisable – like a man in a brash blazer who insists on talking to you in the bar. They have become *passé*. Finally, *Arundo donax*: a huge, jungly, bamboo plant. Marvellous if you want to practise hacking your way through to Tarzan's place but somewhat overpowering in a little city garden.

tulips and it can all go terribly wrong with brash, wholly Non-Yew mixtures of bright colours. Rosemary Verey cleverly uses long, parallel rows of red tulips (the variety is called 'Apeldoorn', in case you want to play safe) in her laburnum walk. It is clever because the danger of a colour clash is totally eliminated. And by using them in the shade of trees, the colour appears less brash.

The most acceptable type of tulip is the sort with a feathered flower. This looks more elegant than the basic oval shape.

Incidentally, tulips are one big exception to the rule that the Yew gardener prefers species plants to hybrids. There is such a grand and exciting tradition of tulip hybrids dating back to the seventeenth century that tulip hybrids are perfectly acceptable.

In general, however, species plants are very much preferred. The Botanic Nursery, referring to dahlias, once suggested that the variety 'Bishop of Llandaff' was 'the only hybrid worth growing'.

The preference for the species is generally expressed as though the Yew gardener likes the plant because of its special qualities which, sadly, get lost in the process of hybridisation. But this is all a front — not to be believed for a second. The real reason the Yew gardener prefers the species is to get away from any possible connection with over-bred plants used by Non-Yew gardeners. The one way to be sure is by having plants which have not been bred at all.

If, most unfortunately, the species plant is positively useless, then the next best thing is a hybrid that was bred as long ago as possible. Hence it is perfectly fine to have *Viburnum x juddii* (a distinct improvement on its species parents) which was raised by William Judd in 1920. But the Yew gardener nervously hesitates to accept the relatively new *Choisya* 'Aztec Pearl' which was created by the nursery, Hilliers, in the 1980s.

In a sense, all this represents a great failure of self-confidence. The Yew gardener seems to cling for dear life to species plants, not daring to risk a taste-disaster by choosing hybrids. It is as though the gardener feared he might be criticised for a plant that was particularly colourful or extravagant. It is as if he were keeping in reserve the defence 'Well, as it happens, this is the original species plant from China brought over by Farrer.'

To be fair, there is also a touch of the Arts and Crafts movement about the preference for the species. The original plant, one could argue, is the 'natural' plant. It is the plant created over millennia by evolution. It is a connection with an unimaginably long botanical history. It is a creation of nature.

Best of all is a *native* species plant. This creates a connection between a garden and centuries of rural Britain. In this category come the Common Dogwood, the Guelder Rose and the Quickthorn (when talking of native plants one tends to used the common instead of the Latin names to emphasise how rural and British they are). None of these native plants would

IS IT YEW TO HAVE VARIEGATED FOLIAGE?

Variegated foliage is a problem. Variegation – by definition – is usually nothing to do with the original species plant. It is usually an aberration of the plant or, in some cases, an affliction since it can be caused by a virus.

So the Yew gardener, in theory, would prefer to have nothing to do with variegated foliage. On the other hand, since the Yew garden is worryingly short of colours and the yew hedge, in particular, is as dark as a stagnant pond, there is a desperate need for any lightening of the gloom. So, after a short internal struggle, the Yew gardener does accept variegated foliage.

But it is done cautiously and in small quantities. Preferably it is done in a way that is as traditional as possible. Standard variegated holly bushes are ideal. Rosemary Verey has some. Say no more.

make much of a garden by themselves. But they can be included to satisfy the desire for a sense of long-established country life.

Similarly, it is terribly Yew to say that you allow plants to seed themselves in your garden. It gives the impression that you love the sense of wild nature surrounding and engulfing you because you yourself, it is implied, have a wild side. This attitude has the added advantage of reducing the workload. You do not have to pull out the self-seeders. It also provides extra colour in the garden which tends – let's face it – to be sorely needed. How many Yew gardens has one gone into which would be miserably dull without the poppies which have invaded and tried to make something of the place.

The guelder rose

One cannot leave Yew plants without mentioning winter scent. Most people quite rightly try to avoid going into the garden in winter at all. Yet Yew gardeners love to maintain the fiction that they are always out there appreciating the subtle scent of viburnums. Among the ones the gardener is supposedly sniffing is *Viburnum farreri* and *Viburnum × burkwoodii*. The Non-Yew gardener smiles cheerfully while being slightly surprised that so much valuable garden space is taken up with these dark and dreary beasts.

NON-YEW PLANTS

The classic Non-Yew planting is hundreds of multi-coloured, double, F1 hybrid petunias (or any other bedding annuals) in a border with hundreds of other multi-coloured, double, F1 hybrid petunias of completely different colours. The idea – in case you have not guessed – is this: to cram in as much blazing colour as humanly possible.

The Non-Yew gardener does not merely *like* colour. He adores it. He longs to gorge himself on it. He is a colour addict. However much you give him, he wants more.

For those who have never seen or heard about truly top-notch Non-Yew planting, the newspaper *Garden News* regularly has pictures of gardens that feature it and gives them prizes. Here is the planting in the front garden of Mr and Mrs Sutton – a garden which has won the *Garden News* Gold Award. It has 350 'non-stop' begonias of varied colours arranged in a circle. Not far away, a 40-gallon plastic orange juice barrel is packed with busy lizzies. This makes a stunning – almost psychedelic – experience. It might be dangerous to visit it while under the influence of drugs.

In all, the whole garden has 1,500 busy lizzies. This is planting on a Victorian scale. The plants are grown from 'plugs' – tiny plants which many seed merchants sell by mail order.

To keep this lot blazing away, the Suttons feed them as though they were a pride of lions. Once a week they get Miracle-Gro – a chemical fertiliser produced by Zeneca. Then they are fed again, during the same week, with Chempak – another chemical fertiliser – to make sure they flower as though their lives depend on it (which they do).

The plants themselves are scientific triumphs. Intensive breeding and selection continually reduces the heights of the stems and increases the exoticism of the colours. Thompson and Morgan produces the biggest seed catalogue in Britain and features amazing inventions such as the dwarf, striped marigold 'Mr Majestic' which has dark brown stripes fanning out from the centre of yellow flowers. From above the pattern looks like the top of a fancy dress hat. It is a curiosity more than anything else. It is deliberately bizarre. It provokes the reaction 'What an extraordinary plant. How strange.'

In the catalogue, Thompson and Morgan goes some way to explain why anyone should want such a plant. The blurb alongside the illustration promises: 'this is definitely something for the neighbours to talk about'. So that is it. The plant is a novelty. It will mark out the gardener who uses it as innovative (other descriptions might come to mind).

But before snobbish gardeners chortle derisively into their Lapsang Souchong, they should be aware of this: many of the creations of the seedsmen are utterly beautiful. Osteospermum 'Weetwood' offered by Elm House Nursery is an elegant white flower with a brown centre. Many of the gazanias offered by Thompson and Morgan have bright but subtle colours and simple shapes. If they were species plants, Yew gardeners would love them to bits.

One of the features of these catalogues is that most plants are sold 'mixed'. The Non-Yew gardener can hardly bear to see one 'colour-way' all on its own. They must be mixed.

On top of this, the Non-Yew gardener wants each individual flower to include within itself two or more colours. The 'T&M Improved Dwarf Mixed

Godetias' are all enthusiastically multi-coloured. There is red with a white stripe, white with a scarlet blob, apricot with yellowish edges, light blue with mauvish edges and so on.

The most artificial-looking confections of all are probably the 'Stripes and Picotees' carnations offered by Thompson and Morgan. These are flowers which have everything you could want (or bear): stripes and picotees, plus the most startling colour combinations.

'Picotees' are little markings on the edges of the petals which make

Busy Lizzies, flowering as though their lives depend on it

them look as though a perfectly good carnation is suffering from a disease. In this case, the stripes and picotees are dark red. The background colours are pretty well any colour you care to think of. Perhaps the flower in this series which requires the most resilient digestive system is the lurid orange-and-red combination. But the full stomach-test only takes place when this is placed next to the yellow-and-red version and the mauvish white-and-red one. It is best not to look at these after a big meal.

At this point it has really become a question of 'what colours would you like, sir?' The seedsmen will make them up for you. Just make your choice and a few years later, it will be provided in any number of colour-ways. This might be artificial. But it cannot be denied that, if the imagination and taste of the buyer is good enough, the results can be wonderful to behold – as many of them are.

Perhaps the feature about Non-Yew plants which Yew gardeners find hardest to bear is the perfection. The pompon shape looks so carefully manicured that any sense of the garden being a place to meet nature totally disappears. One might as well be in a gallery in which are hung many little pictures of abstract art.

The series of asters 'Pompon Splendid Mixed' mostly feature three colours on each flower. By having three colours each in a collection of different colour-ways, in a form which is disturbingly perfect, these must rank among the most thorough-going Non-Yew plants ever manufactured.

The pompon shape

But there is one feature of Non-Yew plants which the Yew gardener finds even harder to bear than the colours: the names.

Yew gardeners would rather cover their patches with concrete than admit their borders contain a begonia called 'Frilly Dilly Mixed'. It would be too, too embarrassing ever to admit to having planted annuals called 'Super Princess Symphonie Mixed', let alone 'Phlox of Sheep' (heaven save us from garden catalogue humour). There is even a sunflower developed by Thompson and Morgan which, without any apparent attempt at irony, has been called 'Pastiche'. One can only assume that the boffins think the word is attractively French and are blissfully unaware of its meaning.

Apart from annuals the most Non-Yew plant is surely pampas grass. As the name suggests, this plant comes from South America. Prominently placed in a front garden, it gives the impression that a gaucho on his battered horse is about to come along any minute – all leather, unshaven face and lopsided, untrustworthy-looking smile. The point – lest it be missed – is that pampas grass does not look as though it could possibly be native to Britain. Rhododendrons can just about get away with their obvious foreignness. At least they are green. But the straw colour of the huge waving pampas grass reveals it as a cowboy plant that has no place in a Yew garden.

Some sharp-eyed observers may object that there is some pampas grass waving about unashamedly in the private garden of Kensington Palace. This does not make the plant Yew. On the contrary, it confirms that pampas grass is Non-Yew since the royal taste is that way inclined (except for the special case of Prince Charles).

The common assumption is that that there is no plant more intensely, absolutely and outstandingly Non-Yew than pampas grass. But there is: *pink* pampas grass. Yes, scientists have reckoned to be able to improve on the straw colour of nature and now offer a pink colour worthy of a Boots eye make-up case. This, surely, is the ultimate, unbeatable Non-Yew plant.

But before finishing, an honourable mention must be made of the whole range of dwarf conifers. All conifers are treated cautiously by snobbish gardeners. They are mostly not in the least bit native. Forests of them in Scotland and elsewhere in Britain are cordially loathed. But special scorn is reserved for dwarf conifers which combine two of the essential elements of Non-Yew plants – they are obviously foreign and they have recently been created by plant breeders. As for a garden made up predominantly of such conifers (in the style of Adrian Bloom) this is utterly Non-Yew. The fact that it provides all-year colour and interest is absolutely comprehensively and rather irritatingly irrelevant.

One tree also deserves special mention. Or is it one tree? It could be two or three. This is the kind which provides two or three different varieties of apple on the same stem. In case one is bored with a glut of Cox's Orange Pippin and then nothing, this tree provides Cox's and then, for variety, some James Grieve. Yew gardeners regard this as naff beyond belief – an interference with the pure naturalness-thingy of the plant. On the other hand, like so many aspects of Non-Yew planting, the idea is terrifically practical.

TOP TEN PLANTS

NON-YEW PLANTS	YEW PLANTS	FASHIONABLE PLANTS

 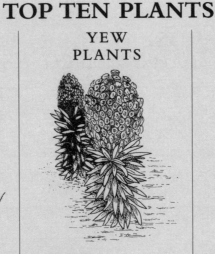 

NON-YEW PLANTS

1. Pink Pampas grass
2. Asters 'Pompon Splendid Mixed'
3. Carnations 'Stripes and Picotees'
4. Ordinary pampas grass
5. Any multi-coloured annuals.
6. Pink narcissi
7. Dwarf Delphiniums
8. Ball-shaped Dahlias.
9. Chrysanthemums (incurved type).
10. Fruit bushes with different varieties on same stem.

YEW PLANTS

1. Euphorbias
2. Alliums
3. Hellebores
4. Viburnums (for winter scent)
5. Roses (species or old varieties)
6. Clematis (species or old varieties)
7. *Corydalis Flexuosa* 'Père David'
8. *Cimicifuga*
9. *Salvia Patens*
10. Daffodils (must be yellow and simple)

FASHIONABLE PLANTS

1. *Cynara cardunculus*
2. Ophiopogons
3. *Miscanthus*
4. Cannas
5. Eryngiums
6. Phormiums
7. *Brassica oleracea* (ornamental cabbage)
8. *Gunnera manicata*
9. *Arundo Donax*
10. *Acanthus spinosus*

'A ROSE BY CERTAIN OTHER NAMES IS NOT AS SWEET'

Roses are grown by both Yew and Non-Yew gardeners. But not the same roses. There is a deep gulf between those roses which are acceptable to the snooty gardener and those which are delightful to everyone else.

The Yew gardener demands old roses: anything you like as long as it was bred before 1900. The Non-Yew gardener, on the other hand, does not mind a jot when the rose was bred. He wants colour, reliability, a long flowering period and other such practical things.

This is precisely what the upmarket gardener used to want too. But his taste has changed.

Gradually, through the middle of the twentieth century, Yew gardeners reached a consensus that the breeding of brighter, more abundant, bigger and longer-lasting flowers had gone too far.

Edward Bunyard in 1936 wrote a book, *Old Garden Roses*, in praise of the more restrained attractions of old varieties. Then Graham Thomas issued a series of books with particular emphasis on old shrub roses. The idea, as he wrote, was to 'bring forth these lovely things from retirement'.

If the name starts off Comte de ... then the rose is authoritatively Yew

All this was, in theory, about the 'proportion of flower size to leaf size and to the bush or tree as a whole'. It sounds purely a matter of aestheticism. But in practice it was about upmarket types being shocked by the vibrant colour-fests that Non-Yew gardeners were creating. They were not restful or restrained and they could not be nostalgic since nothing like them had ever been seen before. The Yew gardener therefore ran away from all modern roses in horror, consigning the whole lot to a mental compost bin.

So it arose that the way for a Yew gardener to be absolutely sure of having a rose 'in good taste' was to buy one that was old and French. If the name starts off Comte de . . . then the rose is authoritatively Yew. If the name begins Madame. . . (anyone), it is elegantly Yew. Gloire de . . . (anywhere) is gloriously Yew. And Souvenir de. . .(anything) is unforgettably Yew.

Yew gardeners are so keen to have these old roses that they sometimes wish their favourite roses were old when in fact they are not. The Royal National Rose Society asks its members which are their favourite old garden roses. The members regularly nominate roses which do not qualify. The members convince themselves of what they wish to believe.

Fantin-Latour: everything the Yew gardener could desire

The most fashionable old rose is currently Fantin-Latour. It has everything the Yew gardener could desire. Its shape is that of a squashed cabbage. Its name evokes the memory of a nineteenth-century French artist. At 6 feet high, it is big enough to be taken seriously without being too big to place. It is a proper, full-grown rose – not a miniaturised freak. It is reasonably close to original species roses. In fact it is a *centifolia*, a kind of rose that was common in the eighteenth century and appeared in paintings as long ago as the sixteenth century. The colour is romantic pink – a gentle pink. It has a sweet scent. Penelope Hobhouse used it at Tintinhull. It practically comes with a guarantee.

Other impressive types of old rose are:

The Gallicas: probably the the oldest of all garden roses, grown by the Greeks and Romans.

The Damasks: another very old group, said to have been brought from the Middle East by the Crusaders.

The Albas: these date back to the Middle Ages, too. Note that their colours are restricted to pink, blush pink and white. Admirable restraint.

And more recently – but still respectably – moss roses, China roses, Portland roses, Bourbon roses and, at a pinch, Hybrid Perpetuals.

The colour is important. Yellow was not easily available in the nineteenth century and so a yellow rose is – by definition – Non-Yew. The favoured colours are pink for the romantics, white for the many who are tremblingly nervous of making a colour clash, and purple or crimson for those who feel rich, dark colours have bags of mystery and no possibility of being brash.

These dark purples and crimsons include Charles de Mills, Cardinal de Richelieu and Mme Isaac Pereire. The whites include Mme Hardy and Mme Plantier. Among the many pinks are Comte de Chambord, Ispahan and Souvenir de Malmaison. Malmaison, incidentally, is where Empress Josephine, the wife of Napoleon, made a famous rose garden, gathering varieties from around the world, blissfully ignoring the fact that her husband was at war with large parts of it. Very Yew.

Cardinal Richelieu: Yew

Another desirable category of rose consists of the

species roses. They represent the ultimate in the Yew gardener's desperate attempt to avoid 'over-bred' roses. They have not been bred at all.

A particularly good one to have is *Rosa Mulligani* . Most people have never heard of it (which is good) and even if they had, they would not have room for it (even better). It is a 'massive grower' but it does its massive growing in the best possible taste by creating flowers that are white and small, gathered in clusters. It is one of the few roses to feature in the gardens of both Rosemary Verey and Penelope Hobhouse. This is a gilt-edged Yew rose.

Bobby Charlton:
Non-Yew

Other good species roses to have are *Rosa moyesii* ('such elegant rosehips') and *Rosa glauca* (otherwise known as *Rosa rubrifolia*) which has leaves with a bluish tinge. But any species rose is safe. Some of them have flowers so sparse and short lived that they could not possibly be vulgar.

Which brings us to roses that could, possibly, provoke the dreaded 'V' word: the Non-Yew roses.

One cannot avoid the names, so let's get them over with: how could anyone with pretensions possibly bear to have a rose called Tequila Sunrise? How could they tell their friends they are growing Baby Love or Sexy Rexy? It is out the question. This is the world of six-packs, Baywatch and films starring Arnold Schwarzenegger. This is Torremolinos-goes-gardening. The Yew gardener instinctively knows he has strayed into foreign territory.

Yew gardeners do not buy roses named after newsreaders, pop singers or footballers. This rules out Angela Rippon, McCartney and Bobby Charlton to name but three. One rose – Peaudouce – was named after a brand of nappy. Even Non-Yew gardeners did not like the whiff of that. Sales improved once it was re-named Elina.

Another thing the Yew gardener does not like about other people's roses is the colour. Yellow is discreetly avoided on the whole. But blue is positively loathed. It is not a natural rose colour – which is precisely why breeders have been trying so hard to create it. It must be admitted that they have not yet been terribly successful. Blue Moon has its faults and has been in part replaced by Blue Parfum. (Please excuse the name. Rose breeders speak Franglais).

Almost as bad are the stripes which appear in certain Non-Yew roses. The stripes of Harry Wheatcroft have to be seen to be disbelieved – they are scarlet and yellow, as though the rose had been tie-dyed by some drug-crazed colour-sadist. The horror which this evokes is – on the other hand – wholly inconsistent since one very Yew rose is striped. It is an old Gallica rose – *Rosa mundi* (also known as *Rosa gallica* 'Versicolor') – which dates back to before 1659. It cannot be accused of being overbred. So, if it is vulgar, then nature is vulgar – a tricky proposition for the Yew gardener.

Rosa 'Harry Wheatcroft'

Similarly there are some old roses which are bi-colour. But this does not stop the Yew gardener from despising modern bi-colour roses. These include Silver Jubilee – pink with tints of peach, one of the most popular roses in the country – and Double Delight – being American, the name actually boasts about the two colours: strawberry and white.

Another thing the Yew gardener dislikes about modern roses is the flower shape. The buds of the modern hybrid tea roses have tight, upright shapes like conference pears wrapped in napkins. The petals open by peeling backwards over themselves which looks – to the Yew eye – about as unnatural as the tail-fins of a 1950s Chevrolet.

The shape of the other major class of modern roses – Floribundas – are better but they still appear artificial to the Yew gardener's eye.

One another thing. Yew gardeners can't bear so-called 'miniature' and 'patio' roses. They find it painful to witness the cramped size of them – like the pinched feet of unfortunate Oriental girls. Angela Rippon is one of them. She is 12" high and is one of those non-colours struggling to be somewhere between red and yellow but ending up nowhere at all.

Why then, you might wonder, does anybody grow modern roses? To put it another way, why do people choose modern varieties for over 80 per cent of the roses they buy? Surely they must have something.

In fact they have so many advantages, it is embarrassing:

1. They have more flowers.
2. They flower repeatedly through the season.
3. The choice of colour is practically unlimited.
4. They are more disease-resistant (not a single old rose features among the top fifteen most healthy roses chosen by members of the Royal National Rose Society).

5. They include some outstanding creations. The shrub rose Graham Thomas is pure yellow, beautifully shaped and fragrant. It is a modern classic. Iceberg is another – pure white with occasional tints of pink. Its flowering is pretty well continuous.

On practical and aesthetic grounds modern roses are hard to exclude altogether. So, in the end, most Yew gardeners relent and admit some of them into their gardens. But you will find they are rather defensive about it. When you visit, the modern roses might not be mentioned at all. Instead, you will be firmly led to the Souvenir de Malmaison – if you chance to go round on one of those rare days when it is in flower.

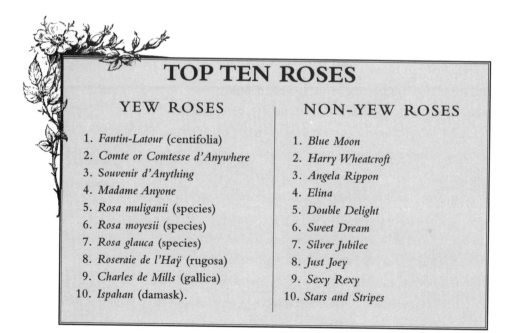

TOP TEN ROSES

YEW ROSES

1. *Fantin-Latour* (centifolia)
2. *Comte or Comtesse d'Anywhere*
3. *Souvenir d'Anything*
4. *Madame Anyone*
5. *Rosa muliganii* (species)
6. *Rosa moyesii* (species)
7. *Rosa glauca* (species)
8. *Roseraie de l'Haÿ* (rugosa)
9. *Charles de Mills* (gallica)
10. *Ispahan* (damask).

NON-YEW ROSES

1. *Blue Moon*
2. *Harry Wheatcroft*
3. *Angela Rippon*
4. *Elina*
5. *Double Delight*
6. *Sweet Dream*
7. *Silver Jubilee*
8. *Just Joey*
9. *Sexy Rexy*
10. *Stars and Stripes*

THE DAHLIA QUESTION

Does a Yew gardener use dahlias? Most gardeners of 'taste' will answer an instant, shuddering and shocked *'No!'*.

These are plants which have been so bred and interbred – with so much incest and perversion thrown in – that most Yew gardeners run from them in horror.

Many dahlias no longer look as though they are plants at all. They do not even look as though they come from planet earth. 'Pompon' dahlias such as Wooton Cupid and Noreen are so perfect and manicured in their little curved petals that they look like those decorations in glass paperweights. Or they could be golf balls from Jupiter or vibrantly coloured Martian droppings.

As if this kind of dahlia was not disturbing enough, there is the 'cactus' sort. Dahlias of this kind look like miniature hedgehogs which have curled up in a ball and been blasted with an electric shock that makes them go pink. Then there are the shaggy flowers called 'decorative' (more in hope than in truth). The 'collerettes' have ruffle collars around the centre – in contrasting colours, of course.

Some of these bizarre creations have been bred so that the flowers reach enormous proportions. The orange Corton Olympic manages blooms of as much as a foot wide. Daleko Jupiter (I am not making this up) has a similarly enormous flower and is often used in exhibitions.

It is a remarkable thing – saying much about the diversity in our culture and the minds of human beings – that such flowers can inspire such utter extremes of admiration and disgust.

Everyone would agree that these flowers are amazing. But the Non-

Yew gardener thinks they are a wonderful triumphs of man and nature combined. The Yew gardener thinks they are a revolting perversion.

Garden News analyses the latest dahlias that have been bred. There are hundreds of them. They are reviewed as seriously (and more enthusiastically) than the latest West End plays. One called Utmost, bred in America, is praised for its 'brilliant bi-coloured blooms with a gold centre and bright red tipping'.

Yew gardeners would run a mile from such creations and, for this reason, they feel safer having nothing to do with dahlias at all. The whole genus is relegated to the no-go area also inhabited by highly bred, highly-multi-coloured chrysanthemums and gladioli.

And yet, and yet. Many well known garden writers have suggested that maybe dahlias should be considered after all. Alan Titchmarsh has suggested that they are on the verge of coming back into fashion. Roy Strong has spoken up for them and quoted the nineteenth-century writer William Robinson doing the same (if being daring it is as well to quote an ancient authority). Christopher Lloyd, having ripped out his rose garden, has included dahlias in the replacement planting. All these writers could be dismissed since they have pages to fill and they habitually like to be provocative. But even the slightly more trustworthy Robin Lane-Fox has spoken in favour of certain specified dahlias (Apricot Jewel, Cherry Wine and, best of all, Dark Splendour).

Now, though, for the litmus test: do Penelope Hobhouse and Rosemary Verey grow them? Yes. In small quantities and without talking about it much, they do.

In Penelope Hobhouse's book on her garden at Tintinhull there is, as previously remarked, a section entitled 'A Passion for Hellebores'. She has no section entitled ' A Desire for Dahlias' (let alone 'A Crush on Chrysanthemums'). She explains that she uses two of them (Bishop of Llandaff and Bloodstone) 'to fill in at the end of the season'. This is not exactly enthusiastic approbation. But it gives a guide to how the Yew gardener can explain away the presence of these plants to a sceptical friend.

Bishop of Llandaff, incidentally, is the most respectable of all the hybrids. In fact it is so respectable it is almost compulsory. But the safest ground to be on – as ever – is to own a species plant. And there is no need for the Yew gardener to worry about which to use. Both Verey and Hobhouse use exactly the same one: *Dahlia merckii*.

Fear of dahlias

GARDEN CENTRES
V
NURSERIES

For the chronically snobbish gardener, no detail is too small to ignore. For such gardeners, the phrase 'garden centre' is spoken with disdain. One does not buy one's plants from mere garden centres. One buys them from 'nurseries'.

Not just any nurseries, either. One buys from specialist nurseries. Some of these are Yew because they specialise in such building blocks of upmarket gardens as topiary, 'architectural plants', hellebores or euphorbias. But the most superior of the superior are nurseries of a particular kind.

Typically they are not open all the time. In case that is not inconvenient enough for you, the catalogue has no pictures. The owner – or one of the owners – goes on plant-finding expeditions to South America, Eastern Europe or the Far East. Ideally he is known – among those who know – as a 'brilliant plantsman'.

When one visits, the place looks so modest that one wonders if one has stumbled into a private house by mistake. There are no gnomes or benches – probably no garden ornaments or furniture or Miracle-Gro for sale at all. At first sight it might seem as though there are no plants either. But in fact the plants are those tiny things with no flowers hiding in the miniature pots.

The real pleasure of such a place is reading the catalogue. The lack of colour pictures is because the plants are only sold in small, select quantities. Instead of pictures, there are phrases to savour such as 'Introduced into cultivation from China by the Compton d'Arcy & Rix expedition of 1988'.

The point of buying at these nurseries is to seek out rare plants. Allow me to translate that sentence: the point of buying at these nurseries is to seek out plants which your friends have not got or even heard of. You look forward to the moment when you will be taking an innocent visitor around your garden and he or she co-operatively says, 'That is an attractive plant. I don't think I recognise it.'

You reply – with an intensity of pleasure rarely experienced out of doors – 'Yes it has done well, hasn't it? It is quite a rare plant recently found by Dan van Hinckelbaum in South America.' Your visitor has walked into the trap and the door has shut with a satisfying 'clunk'.

Your pleasure rises even higher if the plant is from an entire genus which people have never heard of. If the genus is not listed in the RHS *Encyclopedia of Plants and Flowers* then you have reached the pinnacle. A recent catalogue of Green Farm Plants, for example, listed a *Poliomintha* and an *Anthriscus sylvestris*. Neither of these is mentioned in the *Encyclopedia*.

Some of the names are so strange and long that one even starts to wonder whether the nursery is making them up. It is reassuring if one can see on the wall of the nursery – displayed discreetly (but not too discreetly) – an array of gold medals awarded at the Chelsea Flower Show. One is at the leading edge of modern plantsmanship. The little things in the pots might be useless garden plants but who cares?

GREEN FARM PLANTS
Phrases from a Yew catalogue:

'A genus unaccountably underused as garden plants'

'Collected by Brian Halliwell'

'Collected in Portugal, at its most westerly distribution point, by John Fielding'

'Rounded up in its Mexican hideaway by obersturmheron Dan Van Hinckelbaum and judged guilty of presuming to be of more than Botanical Interest Only [sic]'

'This now legendary plant from Phyllis Barwood's garden is very much more than just a collector's item'

'A few divisions to spare'

TOP TEN YEW NURSERIES

1. Green Farm Plants, Surrey (uncommon shrubs, perennials, alpines)
2. Blackthorn Nursery, Hampshire (choice perennials, shrubs and Alpines)
3. Washfield Nursery, Kent (supplies Prince Charles's house 'Highgrove' with hellebores)
4. Crûg Farm Plants, Gwynedd, Wales (new introductions from the Far East, regarded by the cognoscenti as 'the nursery for the twenty-first century')
5. Hadspen Garden and Nursery, Somerset (herbaceous, old-fashioned and shrub roses)
6. Glebe Cottage Plants, North Devon (hard-to-find perennials)
7. Langley Boxwood Nursery, Hampshire (box hedging and topiary)
8. Goldbrook Plants, Suffolk (*hosta, hemerocallis* and bog iris)
9. The Bluebell Nursery, Derbyshire (uncommon trees, shrubs and climbers).
10. Highfield Hollies, Hampshire (standard and other shaped hollies)

NON-YEW SUPPLIERS

1. Bakker (sells bright pink pampas grass)
2. Mr Fothergill's (offers *chrysanthemum carinatum* 'Annual Tricolor' with rings of colour like catherine wheels)
3. D.T.Brown (busy lizzies 'Blackpool Rock' and 'Mega Orange Star')
4. Grooms ('patio packs' of mixed hyacinths)
5. J.Parker (mixed, miniature gladioli with florets 'like the wings of a butterfly')
6. Blackmore and Langdon (offers *Begonia* 'CanCan' – yellow with red frill edging on huge 8-inch-wide blooms)
7. Bressingham Gardens (range includes dwarf conifers)
8. Elm House Nursery (like many Non-Yew suppliers, speaks fluent Franglais: *Verbena* 'Pink Parfait')
9. Thompson and Morgan (biggest seed merchant; offerings include asters 'Pompon Splendid Mixed')
10. Any DIY store (if it sells there, everyone's got it)

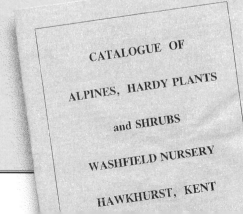

CATALOGUE OF

ALPINES, HARDY PLANTS

and SHRUBS

WASHFIELD NURSERY

HAWKHURST, KENT

1996 Catalogue

Elm House

NURSERY

The Young Plant Specialists

NEW! Wessex Eclipse p.3

NEW! Radiant Lynn p.8

NEW! Pastel Pink p.23

CHAPTER FOUR

DOES ONE GROW VEGETABLES?

N
ot long ago, it was utterly Non-Yew to grow vegetables. The very word 'vegetables' conjured up images of allotments, corrugated iron and mulching with black plastic. The Non-Yew gardener could proceed with his healthy, innocent food-growing without any competition from the smart set.

But not any more. Vegetable growing is now terribly fashionable. Rosemary Verey and Penelope Hobhouse both do it. *Gardens Illustrated* has features about superior vegetables, fruit or herbs in almost every issue.

Of course, this does not mean the superior gardener has acquired a patch in the allotment. A few fashionable journalists might do this but, no, the Yew gardener still does not have a vegetable patch at all. He has a 'kitchen garden' or, better still, a *potager*.

A kitchen garden or *potager* is quite different from a vegetable patch. The first difference is that is laid out as smartly – or even more smartly – than the flower garden. It has old brick paths in geometrical shapes. It has straight lines of hedging (yew for the high hedges, box, lavender or catmint for the low). Even more noticeable is the remarkable number of flowers. In theory we are talking about a place where vegetables are grown. But in practice, the flowers seem to be the things that catch the eye. Are there any excuses for this?

A *potager* is quite different from a vegetable patch

Of course. History. The leaders of Yew gardening have been ferreting among their old texts and found a way to explain why their vegetable patches are a bit short on those vegetable things.

'As in the kitchen gardens of the past,' writes Penelope Hobhouse, 'seasonal flowers from fruit trees and in borders have a strong influence on its general character.' You can say that again, Penelope. There were about a hundred different flowering plants in your so-called kitchen garden at Tintinhull.

As for the 'kitchen garden' you helped with at Royaumont in the Île de France, the photograph in your book does not reveal a single vegetable. Your commentary on the photo mentions that 'fruit trees have been trained as espaliers and honeysuckles grow on wooden trellis pillars'. Very nice, Penelope, but what about the main crop potatoes?

Rosemary Verey, meanwhile, explains the huge volume of flowers in her *potager* in true Yew style: 'Looking back, I realise it was William Lawson [a seventeenth-century writer in case you did not know] who inspired me to change our vegetable patch from its utilitarian rows of carrots, cabbages, Brussels sprouts, potatoes and leeks into a decorative *potager*, where, in his words, "comely borders with herbs" and "abundance of roses and lavender yield much profit and comfort to the senses".'

With these words ringing in her ears, she made a *potager* with rows of purple lavender, eight rose standards (the variety is 'Little White Pet'), straight paths of old brick, balls of box at the corner of each bed, more box shaped into pyramids, two arbours, white painted seats, an eight-arch tunnel and 'wishing to emulate La Quintinie at the *Potager du Roi* at Versailles', four apple trees at the centre of each square bed 'trained into goblet shape'.

Both these gardeners emphasise that height is terribly important in a *potager.* Vegetables, you understand, have this irritating drawback of tending to be rather low. In fact, some of them are actually underground – as low as you can get. So height must be created by fair means or foul. In a frank moment, Rosemary Verey once confessed to putting up bean poles even when she had not yet actually planted beans.

Bean poles for height, *and beans,* at Tintinhull!

One can imagine someone trying to create a terribly upmarket *potager* and feeling, when all the work was completed, that there was something missing. In the end, after walking round and round the garden and re-reading the great authorities of the past, the missing element would come to mind. Ah yes, vegetables.

Why is the kitchen garden so fashionable? In the nineteenth century, any self-respecting aristocratic country house automatically had one because it made sense. The produce was of a comparable cost to that which could be bought in shops. And the times of glut did not matter since the household was big and could absorb sudden large quantities or convert them into preserves.

Then, after the First World War, the cost of both gardening labour and income tax rose. As landlords became relatively poorer, former professional gardeners found they could earn more in the town. Kitchen gardens no longer made financial sense. They died out.

The recent renaissance is down to three factors:

First, they are now such economic nonsense that you have got to have money to compost to afford a full-size kitchen garden. What could be more prestigious than that?

Second, supermarket fruit and vegetables are so tasteless that there is a genuine taste advantage in growing your own.

Third, Yew people have visited in increasing numbers the *potager* to beat all *potagers* at Villandry in the Loire Valley (see box). They have seen how smart a *potager* can be.

One might as well mention the vegetables themselves. A small, select band of Yew gardeners take this far enough to care about the varieties they grow. The

Flowers in the 'Kitchen Garden' at Tintinhull

VILLANDRY

The garden at Villandry has made vegetables respectable. One visit is enough to transform the attitude of the garden snob. Instead of associating cabbages with plastic cloches, he suddenly starts thinking of them as smart, dramatic elements in the garden of an aristocratic home.

Villandry is a Renaissance château that is altogether different from every other château in the Loire valley. The stone building itself is gently romantic. But the notable feature is the extraordinary kitchen garden. The size alone is impressive. It is 12,500 square metres (or, more inaccurately, about the size of two football pitches). The lay-out is strictly formal. The square space is divided into nine smaller squares – like the plan for a game of noughts and crosses.

Generously wide, straight, pea-shingle paths divide these squares. Six soldiers could march along, side by side. The edges of the nine squares are marked by low trellis fencing and step-over apple trees. At the four intersections, large, rustic arbours are covered by climbing roses and honeysuckle.

The nine squares are all subdivided into different geometric patterns using double-width, miniature box hedges. Height is provided by standard roses (red). At the entrances to each of the nine squares are little pieces of woodwork that look rather like bass clefs.

Already impressed by the structure of the place, one then sees the vegetables themselves. They are astonishingly smart.

The beet surges out of the ground with its deep red stems and large crinkled leaves. The cabbages boast an astonishing array of colours including one variety which looks like a white football. Another variety comes in an intense electric grey/blue. In dramatic contrast there are shocking red pimentos and bloated orange gourds. This garden of vegetables is more colourful than most people's flower gardens. And each vegetable is planted in solid blocks to make an emphatic statement.

This remarkable garden was created – though the French do not go on about this – by a Spaniard: Doctor Carvallo. It has influenced hundreds of Yew gardeners including Prince Charles.

The most common criticism is that Villandry is not really a kitchen garden at all. Some Yew gardeners complain it is obviously all arranged for visual effect rather than food production. They are shocked at such shamelessness. British Yew gardeners at least *pretend* their vegetables are for eating.

preferred ones, naturally, are those that are rare or ancient. Ideally they should look as knobbly as possible to show that they were not bought at a supermarket. A *Gardens Illustrated* feature on a kitchen garden showed 'Pink Fir Apple' potatoes which would be a promising contestant in a knobbly vegetable competition. Perfect. Or rather, perfectly imperfect.

The pursuit of the rare and edible is helped by the Henry Doubleday Research Association which tries to find obscure or forgotten varieties. Subscribing members are offered limited numbers of seeds which can be obtained from nowhere else. This sort of thing is ideal.

Similarly with fruit trees, the Yew gardener is not obliged to care too much about which varieties he grows. Apple and pear trees are such major contributors to the look of one's kitchen garden that they do not need to do any more to earn their keep. They contribute height, blossom and formal shapes including espaliers and step-over hedges – as at Monet's garden in Giverny. Any actual fruit is an unexpected bonus.

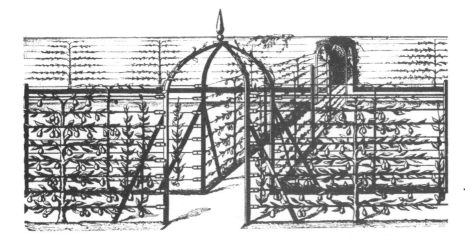

Espaliers contribute height, blossom and formal shapes. Any actual fruit is an unexpected bonus.

But if one chooses to care, one prefers the rare and old varieties. One says that supermarkets only stock those apples and pears which store and handle well and produce a large weight from each tree, whereas one's own priorities are taste and an interest in history. A gardener quoted in *Gardens Illustrated* recommended 'old-fashioned' dessert varieties such as Whinham's Industry for their 'extra flavour' while admitting that they were 'more prone to mildew'. Quite.

The other sort of vegetable the Yew gardener grows is the sort that looks almost as good as a flower. A classic among this sort of vegetable is kohlrabi which can have large light blue leaves with red veins. Certain varieties of beet can be excitingly red. Actually eating these things is purely optional.

This sort of cavalier attitude, however, will certainly not be found in the Non-Yew gardener's allotment. Here a completely different approach prevails.

The Non-Yew gardener expects his vegetables to perform. Looks are secondary. The Non-Yew will use any method – improvised, extravagant or absurd – to get results.

Medwyn Williams, for example, uses sawn-off oil drums for growing his competition carrots. Mel Ednie is the world champion onion grower. To achieve his elevated status, he used heating pipes, a 'dibbler' specially made for him, black and white polythene sheets, a porous pipe system, a reverse thermostat, the systemic insecticide Benlate (no longer manufactured, he says with regret), plastic-coated wire rings and a tape measure. A 3kW fan heater was positioned along the middle path in his tunnel to maintain the air temperature at 13C. And four high-pressure sodium lamps were spaced along the beds and left on for 10 hours a day for three weeks.

This does not resemble gardening so much as D-Day. It is a military campaign, thought out to the last detail. The result – which broke the world record – was an onion weighing 15lb 15½ ounces (7.26 kilos). It was almost the size of a football.

Feeding such monsters is all-important. Dave Smith from Eckington, Sheffield, grows his carrots in a mixture made of a bucket of silver sand, another of peat and another of vermiculite. To this he adds three ounces of superphosphate, another three of lime and another three of potash. His carrots have no choice but to grow.

The pleasure that some Non-Yew gardeners get from their vegetable-growing is genuinely enviable. For them, each Spring brings the excitement of starting on a brand new process of creation. The year will be satisfyingly productive not just decorative.

Bernard Ostler, who writes for *Garden News*, started one of his columns: 'I woke up with a feeling of excitement – cultivating day had arrived.'

BIGGEST
FAUX PAS

He fed the birds, opened the vents in the greenhouse and then got down to the main business: 'As I set up the cultivator and filled the tank with petrol, I began to feel that the new season was really getting under way.'

The cultivator barked into life. 'The machine had been serviced the previous autumn' (Gertrude Jekyll would have approved). 'For the next few hours I was in a world of my own with just the noise of the engine for company.' What delight he obviously feels when he says, 'At times, the machine was almost buried itself as the soil was broken down into a fine tilth'. 'Eventually, the job was done,' he wrote. 'I was ready for a brew and a well-earned rest.'

He also enjoys the companionship of the allotment – something which the Yew gardener will never know. 'Pete' asks him what he will doing next and Bernard tells him – perhaps at greater length than 'Pete' had bargained for. It involved Growmore, raking down, sterilising, marking out, sowing, planting and more.

These people could bore at Olympic standard but my goodness they know their stuff.

HERB GARDENS

Herb gardens are very Yew. Sissinghurst has one. So does Villandry. Rosemary Verey's high class customers have probably asked her to design more herb gardens than anything else. One of them asked for a herb garden as a present for his wife. It had to be designed and planted within a week.

Herb gardens have the delicious scent of history about them. William Lawson in his book *The Country Housewife's Garden* (published in 1618) mentioned lavender, wall germander, rock hyssop and lavender cotton. With a background like that, an Elizabethan knot garden with low hedges of clipped herbs set in gravel cannot fail to be Yew.

The historical allure goes back even further: to Roman times. One specialist nursery, Hexham Herbs, has created a small Roman herb garden to display the varieties that would have been grown during the occupation of Britain. Such a garden, would have been in the central courtyard of the house with fruit trees, statues and perhaps a fountain. The Yew gardener likes nothing better than to position himself at the end of 2,000 years of history. It is a bonus that, historically, herb gardens were associated with monasteries or the homes of the wealthy. Yew gardeners don't a bit mind associating themselves with the pious or the rich either.

Herbs, to be brutal, tend to be low and green.

Another association Yew gardeners rather like is the way herbs have been used for millennia for cooking and medicinal purposes. According to Gerard, writing in 1596, sage (*Salvia officionalis*) is good for 'taking away shakey trembling of the members'.

But if one cuts through all these delightful historical overtones, perhaps the main reason why herb gardens are so Yew is that they are so sober. You have to work very hard to get enough colour into a herb garden to make it garish. Thyme and parsley and chives tend to be pretty tame creatures – unlikely to frighten the horses. Which leads to the main problem with herb gardens: they are dull. The one at Sissinghurst is a discreet yawn. Even the much more interesting herb garden at Villandry is a let-down after the vegetable garden below. Herbs, to be brutal, tend to be low and green. The more authentically historical they are, the less colourful. They mark the point at which Yew restraint finally goes too far and reaches tedium.

CHAPTER FIVE

HEDGES AND TREES

X

Anyone wanting to plant an upmarket hedge has numerous options. The choice is vast. You can have any hedge you like – as long as it's yew. Practically every well-known garden in Britain has yew hedging. Hidcote has it. So has Great Dixter, Hatfield House, Sissinghurst, Holdenby House, Levens Hall (notably) and many others. Barnsley House, Tintinhull and Howick Hall have it, too.

It is not actually compulsory. But making an upmarket garden without yew hedging is like baking a cake without flour or going to France without crossing the Channel. It is possible. But why try?

It was not always so. John Evelyn, the celebrated seventeenth-century diarist, started the fashion. At least he claimed that he did and garden historian Miles Hadfield believes him. Evelyn commended yews for 'braving all the efforts of the most rigid winter'. He admired them for being evergreen and beautiful. He commended them for use as 'standards, knobs, walks, hedges etc., in all which works they succeed marvellous well'. In view of all these qualities,

Biddulph's Grange c. 1920

he argued, they are 'worth our patience'. Everybody knows what he meant by that: yew is dreadfully, miserably, painfully slow-growing.

Of course, that adds to the prestige. The slow growth deters most people from growing it at all. So yew hedges are always rare and always old. That is why yew will always be Yew.

It is true there are other kinds of hedge, apart from yew, which do not actually disgrace a household. Beech is all right. It is an old, native tree. The browning of its leaves in winter keeps the nature-loving gardeners among us happily in touch with the

yew hedges are always rare and always old. That is why yew will always be Yew.

passing of the seasons. The retention of those leaves means the owners preserve some privacy.

Holly is even better when it comes to being a part of an ancient British heritage. Not only is it celebrated in the carol 'The Holly and the Ivy' but John Evelyn wrote a famous eulogy to it (well, it is famous among garden historians). Evelyn wrote, 'Is there under Heaven a more glorious and refreshing object of the kind, than an impregnable hedge [of holly] of about four hundred foot in length, nine foot high, and five in diameter which I can show in my now ruined gardens at any time of the year, glittering with its armed and varnished leaves?'

The trouble – despite this famous eulogy – is that holly has few advantages over yew. It does have berries. But it is slow-growing and dark, just like yew. And unlike yew, it cannot be cut into precise shapes.

Hornbeam is another possibility. If it is good enough for the wide avenue at Hidcote, it is good enough for any of us.

Also at Hidcote there is a 'tapestry' hedge – that is one made of a mixture of different plants, preferably all selected from the above list, plus purple beech. It is rather an odd thing, a tapestry hedge, since the mixture destroys the smartness. If there is any advantage at all, it is that the tapestry breaks up the monolithic feeling which a large yew hedge can create.

An old country hedgerow is also acceptable. Ideally this should be very old, dating back to Saxon times. Hedgerows are supposed to add a new species of plant every hundred years. So the more species, the better. It is also quite fashionable to start off new 'Saxon' hedges of mixed plants. This can be said with confidence since Rosemary Verey has started off such a Saxon hedge for Prince Charles at Highgrove. Informal hedgerows and Saxon hedges should not, of course, be anywhere near the house. These are for the outlying acreage.

Nearest the house should be a completely different type of hedge – the low, formal one. This is almost invariably made of box or dwarf box (*Buxus sempervirens* 'Suffruticosa'). It runs along the edge of flower beds or creates knot-gardens. Rosemary Verey suggests, incidentally, that the knots in a knot garden should be cut so that the hedge appears to go under and over itself. This gives a sense of movement, she says. Not a bad idea. Otherwise one might, on the contrary, have rather a strong sense of nothing happening at all.

One might also want a less formal hedge of, say, a species rose. But the preferred low, informal hedge is lavender. That is what Gertrude Jekyll often used.

After all these well-behaved and generally slow-growing hedges, it comes as a bit of a shock to meet the king of the Non-Yew hedges: *x Cupressocyparis leylandii*. It stands above them all – literally. It grows like a rocket. One can expect three feet a season. Starting from scratch, one can

Knots from Gervase Markham

TOPIARY

Topiary is very Yew. It goes back to the Romans. It speaks and reeks of centuries of garden history. The newly restored Privy Garden at Hampton Court has yew pyramids and holly standards (a ball of foliage on top of a straight, bare stem).

Hundreds of superior gardens – new and old – have topiary. Hidcote has it, so do Seaton Delaval House, Mapperton House in Dorset, Hatfield House, Renishaw Hall in Derbyshire, Great Dixter and most emphatically of all, Levens Hall in Cumbria.

But not all types of topiary are Yew. A tall pyramid or standard is certainly Yew. But a plant cut into the shape of a peacock or chicken is borderline. A plant in the shape of a teapot, space rocket, car or telephone is definitely Non-Yew. The superior gardener takes his garden seriously.

The best shapes and sizes are those which are slightly unusual yet unquestionably sober. Rosemary Verey has an avenue of yews which are cut like the outline of flower vases. Penelope Hobhouse is growing a short avenue

Levens Hall c1920

Bradfield, Devon c1920

of very tall yew pyramids. Since the plants are relatively young, it will take decades before her plan is complete. She does not even know whether she will live to see the day. This kind of long-term thinking is very Yew. It is gardening as a defiance of mortality.

The kind of plant one uses is important. The more slow-growing, the better. Yew, naturally is outstanding. Holly is good and perhaps even more historic. Box is fine. But it is a distinct step down to bay. A standard bay can cost the price of an opera ticket if bought at a certain smart London garden centre. But it can also be bought at Homebase and large branches of Sainsbury at bargain basement levels. When a garden feature is so popular that Sainsbury sells it, its social status is under threat. Yew gardening cannot remain Yew unless carried out by a choice minority. Otherwise it would fail to fulfil its function: differentiating those who wish to be differentiated.

screen off one's noisome neighbours in a mere three years. The price to be paid is the bother (or expense) of keeping this Triffid under control. It needs to be pruned twice a year to keep the top anywhere close to human beings.

Leylandii is one of the great hate plants of upmarket gardeners. They loathe it for getting too big. They loathe it for being planted by horticultural ignoramuses. They loathe it for being foreign. But above all, they loathe it for being utterly and unbearably common. It is available everywhere – especially in the countryside where people are desperately trying to get rid of the sight of each other. It is available in all sizes and with several variations. There is a gold version. Arguably this is even more Non-Yew, but at least, when it gets out of control, it is not quite as dark.

After this peak of Non-Yewness, it is rather a anti-climax to descend to the other Non-Yew hedges whose main offence is merely to be too jolly. *Eleagnus ebbingei* 'Limelight' is variegated and bright. It does not become enormous and is useful for a town front garden. Much bigger – and also variegated and bright – is spotted laurel. It is easy to grow. Dear, oh dear.

TREES

When it comes to trees, there is civil war between two opposing factions of Yew gardeners. These factions can be polite enough to each other at dinner parties provided the subject of trees – like religion and politics – is avoided. But once trees are mentioned, bitter insults are hurled across the table. The warring parties can be divided into the 'idealists' and the 'realists'.

The idealists passionately believe that large woodland trees are the only 'proper' trees. Stephen Lacey, the Oliver Cromwell of this party, argues that even built-up cities look best with large, majestic trees. Already we are getting some idea of how they feel about trees. Note the words 'large' and 'majestic'.

Lacey puts forward his arguments as though it were a matter of logic. It is all to do with proportion, he says. Big trees suit big town houses, he

The Physick Garden at Chelsea.

Cedars of Lebanon at the Physic Garden Chelsea

argues. Presumably big trees also suit the wide open countryside, too. But the truth is, logic has nothing to do with it. The idealists simply love big trees. They adore them. They hug them. Hugging a dwarfed little pear tree just would not be the same. I suspect that Prince Charles is one of the idealist sort. He bought Highgrove not, as you might think, because he liked the house. He bought it because he adored the tree. At the back, Highgrove has a massive Cedar of Lebanon. Once the Prince saw it, he probably trembled at the knees and the house hunt was over.

Gertrude Jekyll was another who got rather more excited than is considered proper among the upper classes when she contemplated trees.

Her first book was called *Wood and Garden*. Note that the 'wood' came before the 'garden'. In one chapter she described in detail how the 'woodman' went about cutting a trunk of oak. She devoted two and a half pages revelling in every detail. It is hard to tell which thrilled her more: the skill of the woodman or the strength of the tree.

The idealists are so hopelessly in love with 'real' trees that they cannot bear to contemplate mere 'decorative' ones. They regard it as a provocation that these 'decoratives' should call themselves trees at all.

Stephen Lacey tears them off a strip and, passion roused, names names. The sort of trees to avoid, he declares, are 'golden robinia, purple-leaved plum and other freakish cultivars'.

This is fighting talk. And he has not finished with them yet. 'They rise, brash and cartoon-like, into the general landscape,' he snarls.

Against this onslaught, the 'realists' are on the defensive. They do not, unfortunately, have trembling passion on their side. They only have realism. They stoutly maintain that although large trees are lovely, they increase the risk of root damage to houses and walls. Big trees create dense shade. If

PLEASE PLEACH ME
∽ cutting trees to shape ∽

Cutting trees into shapes is very Yew. Cutting them to make an umbrella (or half-ball) shape is a long-established idea. You can see May trees cut into this shape in front of the east façade of Kensington Palace.

But the most beloved form of tree shaping is 'pleaching'. For those not familiar with the term, pleaching consists of planting trees in a row and then trimming them so that the foliage becomes like a sort of hedge on sticks.

The attractions of pleaching are that it is formal, smart and relatively rare (in Britain). Therefore anyone wishing to add a touch of class to his garden needs look no further.

Hidcote has an avenue of pleached trees. The avenue is short, but it is so smart that it is repeatedly photographed. The celebrated garden designer Russell Page often incorporated pleached trees, especially in combination with yew hedges. There is an example of this at Longleat. Rosemary Verey has a little avenue of pleached trees, too.

The French – for whom smartness is all – adore pleaching. The Place des Vosges – the oldest and perhaps loveliest square in Paris – is pleaching, pleaching all the way. The Palace of Versailles shows the heights which pleachomania can reach. There are avenues, hundreds of yards of avenues, with pleached trees all the way along.

Some people – practical, Non-Yew people – might object that pleaching does not create an effective screen. The foliage does not reach the ground, so as a screen, it is completely useless. It can be undermined simply by bending down.

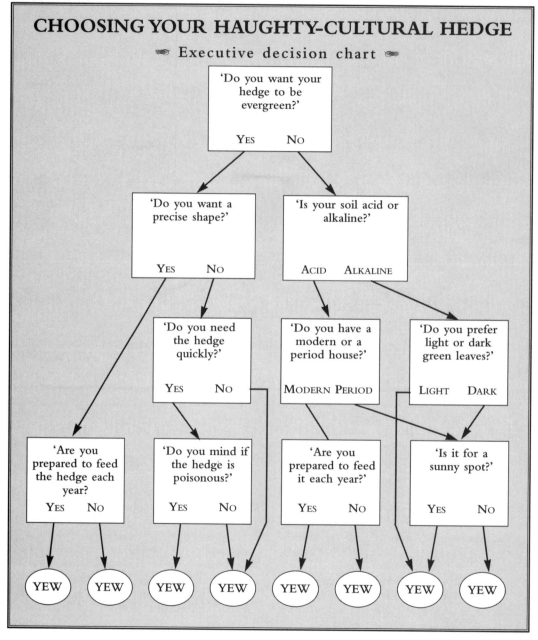

CHOOSING YOUR HAUGHTY-CULTURAL HEDGE

❦ Executive decision chart ❦

'Do you want your hedge to be evergreen?'

YES   NO

'Do you want a precise shape?'

YES   NO

'Is your soil acid or alkaline?'

ACID   ALKALINE

'Do you need the hedge quickly?'

YES   NO

'Do you have a modern or a period house?'

MODERN   PERIOD

'Do you prefer light or dark green leaves?'

LIGHT   DARK

'Are you prepared to feed the hedge each year?'

YES   NO

'Do you mind if the hedge is poisonous?'

YES   NO

'Are you prepared to feed it each year?'

YES   NO

'Is it for a sunny spot?'

YES   NO

YEW YEW YEW YEW YEW YEW YEW YEW

provoked further, realists might add that most big woodland trees do not flower well or do anything particularly interesting at all. The field maple – which Lacey suggests is native and honest – is one of the most boring trees in Britain.

But realists do feel a bit guilty about their little trees. So they make an extra effort to make sure that at least they plant the 'right sort'.

The agreed first choice is not even particularly little. It is magnolia. Penelope Hobhouse adores magnolias. Even Stephen Lacey likes them if the spot is cramped enough.

Some cherry trees are all right. They must be relatively large – like 'Tai Haku' – or else useful – like the winter-flowering cherry (*Prunus subhirtella* 'Autumnalis').

Crab apples are safe. They are native and the flowers are suitably modest. One appreciates them for their fruit and perhaps their autumn colour. *Malus tschonoskii* is favoured. If you can say that you grow crab apples to make jelly, it makes up for a lot.

The ground becomes distinctly more dangerous as one moves towards the sorbuses. Rosemary Verey has plenty of them. But Penelope Hobhouse at Tintinhull grew only one. They can be very decorative. Too decorative, perhaps.

Which brings us to the trees which have, undeniably, crossed the invisible line – the ones which are certifiably Non-Yew. The golden robinia (*Robinia pseudoacacia* 'Frisia' and others similar) is a classic Non-Yew tree. The golden robinia offends by the smallness of its leaves and its happy, garish colour. It is also far too popular.

Nearly all gold-coloured trees are Non-Yew. Less definitely, purple-leaved trees are Non-Yew too. But what is really unbearable is the way that different coloured trees are sometimes brought together. The Non-Yew gardener believes he is making a dramatic and exciting colour statement by combining trees with blue leaves, gold leaves and purple leaves. But there is a danger in such gardens of phrases such as 'dog's dinner' irresistibly erupting from one's mouth.

Also disliked are trees which look foreign even though they are, in fact, no more foreign than the Cedar of Lebanon (consistency is not a strong point among Yew gardeners). Acers with highly divided leaves look far too oriental. They would look all right in a Japanese garden, so it is thought, but the delicate lace effect does not harmonise with the great macho leaves of, say, the British lime.

Many conifers are beyond the pale, especially dwarf ones. The conifer which upmarket gardeners most dislike is a golden pillar such as *Chamaecyparis lawsoniana* 'Elwood's Gold'. The gold colour adds an extra element of unnaturalness to the foreignness.

The queen of the suburbs: cherry 'Kanzan'.

The tree most guilty of looking foreign is the eucalyptus. It normally has particularly foreign-looking bluish leaves in a straggly habit above a trunk which looks like the stripes of a stretched zebra or the camouflage markings on a tank.

But the tree which takes the prize as the most Non-Yew tree of all goes to one which is small, decorative and has blossom that is far too bright. The flowers are double as well as being a strong pink. This is the top one – the queen of the suburbs: cherry 'Kanzan'.

ESSENTIAL TREES

YEW HEDGES	NON-YEW HEDGES	LARGE UPMARKET TREES	SMALLER UPMARKET TREES	NON-YEW TREES
1. Yew	1. Leyland Cypress	1. Cedar of Lebanon	1. Magnolia (any sort)	1. *Prunus* 'Kanzan' (too bright)
2. Beech	2. Golden Leyland Cypress	2. *Quercus ilex* (the ever-green or 'Holm' oak)	2. *Prunus subhirtella* 'Autumnalis' (and most other, but not all, cherries)	2. Eucalyptus (too foreign)
3. Holly	3. *Eleagnus ebbingei* 'Limelight'	3. Walnut (*'Every garden should have a walnut'* – Rosemary Verey)	3. *Malus tschonoskii* (and most other crab apples)	3. *Robinia pseudoacacia* 'Frisia' (too golden)
4. Hornbeam (like beech but different)	4. Spotted laurel	4. Scotch Pine (preferably in Scotland)	4. *Sorbus hupehensis*	4. *Prunus* 'Amanogawa'
5. 'Tapestry' mixture of any of above.	5. Queen Elizabeth roses	5. Beech (in a wood)	5. *Corylus avellana* 'Contorta' (a hazel).	5. Silver birch.
6. Lime – for rows of pleached trees.	6. *Thuja* 'Emerald'			6. Variegated willow grafted to make a standard.
7. Box – for low hedges	7. Lawson cypress 'Golden Wonder'			7. *Rhus typhina* ('Stag's Horn')
8. Long-established country hedgerow (the more species the better)	8. Privet			8. *Acer palmatum atropurpureum*
9. 'Saxon' hedge.	9. Rose 'The Fairy'			9. Any golden conifer.
10. Lavender (Gertrude Jekyll used it)	10. *Euonymus*			10. Purple plum

Cedar of Lebanon

CHAPTER SIX
GOOD BONES

PATHS, PATIOS, BENCHES, CHAIRS, ARCHES, WALLS, POTS AND PAINT

Everybody is more aware of unfair discrimination these days. We are painfully conscious of racism, sexism, fatism and ageism. In upmarket gardening, there is a similar deplorable discrimination. It is ageism, again. But the other way round. Over and over again, the new is ruthlessly shunned in favour of the old.

Take brick paths. Brick paths are, in general, thoroughly acceptable to the superior gardener. They are widespread in gardens designed by Sir Edwin Lutyens. They are traditional and British. This is safe ground on which to stand. But how much better, it is thought, to have paths made of *old* bricks. New bricks, frankly, are treated like second class citizens. This remarkable preference is not covert or discreet at all. People are quite brazen about it.

Rosemary Verey unashamedly complains, 'I can't tell you how

> NO
> HAWKERS,
> DOGS OR
> NEW
> BRICKS

difficult it is to find old bricks.'

The same prejudice in favour of the old applies to benches. At Sotheby's auction sales, cast iron seats made by Coalbrookdale in the nineteenth century fetch three or four times the price of mid-twentieth-century ones designed by the artist Edward Bawden. The Coalbrookdale designs are over-the-top renditions of nasturtiums and the like. If they were new, they would be regarded as naff. But they are old. So they benefit from this pervasive ageism. Bawden benches are more elegant. But what can one say? They are unbearably twentieth century.

Where does this passion for age come from? Everyone has a different theory. My own is that it is all to do with a loss of self-confidence among the upper classes – loss of empire, decline of aristocratic inheritances though taxation and so on. This has caused them to cling to the past in any form. At least with the past, you know what you are getting.

Coalbrookdale benches benefit from pervasive ageism.

Reinforcing 'loss of Empire' insecurity is the Arts and Crafts belief that materials should be what they appear to be. Wood should look like wood, stone like stone and nothing, in turn, should pretend to be wood or stone.

Such are the prejudices and attitudes of the Yew gardener as he approaches the bones of a garden – the basic elements. These bones differentiate the Yew gardener from the Non-Yew even more than the plants. The upmarket rules on them are alarmingly definite.

CHAIRS AND BENCHES

The most reliably upmarket bench is made of hardwood in a simple, sturdy design. To be safely Yew, the bench should be boring. The trouble with interesting benches is that they get noticed. Once they are noticed, it might be observed by one's 'friends' that the 'interesting' design of a few years ago has become passé. This fate is now overcoming Chinese Chippendale style benches. The Lutyens style, too – even though less frequently bought – is far too easily recognisable.

A stone bench, however, is securely superior. As a practical object it is useless. It is cold to sit on and some kinds of stone cling remorselessly to moisture, ensuring that anyone who sits on them will get a damp bottom regardless of whether or not rain has fallen in the past few days. The shape is certain to be uncomfortable. All these inconveniences reinforce the status of stone benches as thoroughly Yew.

An iron-work chair or bench is almost as smart. It is very cold to sit on but it does not hold water so tenaciously. A few hours after rain, a cushion can be placed on top of the seat. This superior practicality forces iron chairs a little lower down the social scale.

On the cusp, between Yew and Non-Yew, are pretend iron-work chairs and benches made of aluminium. These are certainly not as Yew as real iron benches because they are copies, not originals. They are also dangerously practical. They are lighter and they do not rust.

Since they cannot be told apart from iron unless one tries to lift them up or scratch them, the Yew gardener might think he can just about get away with them. But beware. Some are so sparse and insubstantial that they shriek 'I am the cheapest possible, aluminium, mock-iron bench bought at B and Q.'

Quite definite in repelling the upmarket gardener is the 'rustic' bench made of softwood shorn of its bark but retaining – or rather vulgarly boasting – of the roundness of its pieces.

But the ultimate Non-Yew garden furniture is, of course, the most comfortable. Nothing is more delightful than to sit in the garden on a reclining chair made of glistening white plastic, strengthened – tastefully out of sight – with bare, tubular aluminium. The springs on the seat provide enormous comfort, enhanced by generous cushions for one's bottom, back and even legs. What repose! What luxury! All this is strictly forbidden to the Yew gardener.

White plastic is not 'natural', it is not traditional, it is easily available in huge do-it-yourself stores at reasonable prices. Clearly it is beyond the pale. While the Non-Yew gardener stretches himself contentedly in an orgy of physical well-being, the Yew gardener must sit on his stiff, wooden bench and suffer for his class.

PATHS, PATIOS AND TERRACES

The Yew gardener's rules for surfaces underfoot are particularly firm. Only natural materials are acceptable especially stone, brick (preferably old), and pea shingle. Naturally the respectablility of these materials is firmly shored up by their substantial disadvantages. Stone is very expensive. Old bricks, as Rosemary Verey says above, are hard to find. And pea shingle makes a crunchy noise whenever you step on it and throws itself from the path on to the lawn, borders and anywhere else it is not wanted.

Heale House: the respectability of stone is shored up by its expense

A path at Dartington Hall: 'only natural materials are acceptable'

What remains? The material that is cheap, practical and comes in all sorts of shapes and sizes: concrete. With all these practical qualities, concrete is utterly Non-Yew. Bare, honest concrete is bad enough. But even worse is concrete cast to look like York stone, with little imitation ridges. The Yew ethos abominates imitation. Pretension loathes pretence.

That is why few objects are more Non-Yew than concrete paving

The Yew ethos abominates imitation. Pretension loathes pretence.

made to look like natural stones in a woodland path. Agriframes sells a mould into which you can pour concrete to make stone-like shapes that have gaps between them. The brochure suggests that the buyer should take the fakery even further and colour his concrete 'stones'. One shudders.

Yet, if it comes to a contest, surely the most Non-Yew path or patio consists of concrete paving slabs of different colours. Cream and red and grey slabs all together are positively ostentatious about their artificiality. A path made with such slabs and edged with 'Victorian style' rope edging terracotta tiles made of ultra-violet stabilised polypropylene would be the ultimate Yew paving nightmare.

ARCHES, ARBOURS AND GATES

In the world of arches, arbours and gates, one name acts as dreadful temptation to Yew gardeners: Agriframes. Agriframes makes arches and other useful objects which can be ordered by making a single telephone call. The kits are delivered promptly. They are easy to erect. They are built to last. And they are discreetly black. Maybe no one will notice! How easy, quick and sensible it would be to contact Agriframes.

Yet the Yew gardener knows in his heart that he must gather his prejudices together and resist. For Agriframes arches, arbours, and so on are made of tubular steel to which 'all-weather black nylon' is 'chemically bonded'. This is a description packed with no-noes.

Instead, the Yew gardener must tread a longer and more difficult path. Rosemary Verey suggests that, when it comes to gates, he should have them especially made to his own design. That means finding an iron foundry willing to undertake a small, one-off project; working out a design for the gate, regardless of any aptitude for such work; sending it off

The Yew gardener must travel a longer and more difficult path to get an estimate; discussing it all with the foundry; arranging delivery; having the thing painted and then having it fixed.

Of course, there is one advantage to all this. It provides practice for the subsequent purchase of an arch.

ROSE SUPPORTS

The Victorians were masters at making large iron rose supports. Monet's garden at Giverny has some wonderful constructions for encouraging roses to grow up the middle and then burst out at the top in a shower of blooms. Agriframes – again – has created something smaller but similar called the 'Parapluie'.

The Non-Yew gardener will find it good value and available in no time at all. The Yew gardener had better get in touch with the foundry again.

Agriframes plant supports: 'all-weather black nylon' is 'chemically bonded'. This is a description packed with no-noes for the Yew gardener.

WALLS AND FENCES

For the Yew gardener, there is a clear pecking order in walls and fences. Ageism rears its imperious head again. The most desirable kind is an ancient wall. A stone wall is ideal but brick or flintstones are excellent too. A good old wall is so important that Penelope Hobhouse chose her current house mostly because of its old walled garden. The extreme desirability of old walls is increased by the fact that they are incredibly expensive to build new. Failing an old wall, a new one will have to do, of course. Ideally it should be made with old bricks.

Fences are far less desirable. The Yew gardener sees them as 'suburban'. It is a pity to use this, the rudest word in the Yew vocabulary, but it cannot be avoided. The only fences that are genuinely Yew are simple agricultural ones – the sort of thing you might see round a paddock or a field consisting simply of two rough-hewn cross bars between the uprights. Also permissible – not too close to the house – is a wattle fence. It is so rustic and traditional that no one can object.

Trellis is allowed, but it should be a substantial wooden one.

For those in town, a trellis is allowed. But it should be a substantial wooden one. Ideally it should be made of hardwood and tailored by a specialist company. Trellising that is skimpy or plastic is no good at all.

The Non-Yew gardener observes all this agonising over walls and fences with utter detachment. For him, they are no problem at all. They don't matter. They will soon be absolutely covered with flowers and will not be visible anyway.

POTS

For the Yew gardener, pots must be made of terracotta, stone, marble or wood.

Terracotta pots are a prominent part of traditional Italian gardening. The Isola Bella in Lake Maggiore is smothered with them, so they are perfectly respectable. Prince Charles has a very large number of pots. In fact he seems even more passionate about pots than he does about trees. He is a potaholic.

But what sort of pots should one have? The greatest danger for the Yew gardener is to go over the top and buy pots with excessively extravagant decorations. These might be all right if the pots are large and the house is grand. But they will be deemed 'inappropriate' if placed in the vicinity of, say, an 'executive home'. It is absolutely vital to pitch one's grandeur at the right level.

The safest bet is the plain pot. But, again, what sort of plain pot? Two kinds have special kudos:

1) The plain pot which one brought back in the boot of one's car from Italy itself, and

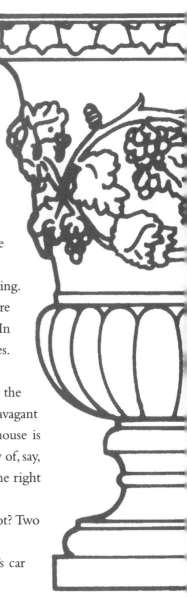

2) You have guessed, the *old* pot. If you have not got an old pot, a superior garden centre – 'The Chelsea Gardener' – is eager to supply you with one.

The most prestigious pots of all are stone ones that have been in one's family for years – huge things, hand-carved by Italian craftsmen. If you have not inherited some of these, Sotheby's or Christie's will, as usual, come to your aid. They have carved stone or marble urns (yes, at the highest level, pots are 'urns') in each of their garden sales. A cheque with four digits before the full stop will probably be required. They have even more supplies of nineteenth-century cast iron urns. Not quite as impressive. But not quite as expensive either.

At the highest level, pots are 'urns'

The Non-Yew gardener, meanwhile, is saving pots of money. He is quite happy to go along with urns, if they are the style of the moment. But his urns certainly do not have to be stone. They don't even have to be cast iron or terracotta. They can just as well be made of good old white plastic.

But, for a change of style, Agriframes offers a 'planter' in the shape of a Tudor-style terracotta chimney pot at Hampton Court. The planter has been cast in 'moulded polypropylene'. Placed next to one of the white plastic Greek urns, the effect is quite remarkable.

The Non-Yew gardener also delights in turning everyday objects into plant containers. A used orange juice barrel; a sawn-off, maxi-size, plastic detergent container or – that classic of Non-Yew planting – the sink. The sink is not left as a sink, though. Time and money is spent coating it with cement. The cement is then coated with yoghurt. Moss and lichen creep over it. The appearance is created of a *stone* sink.

The most traditional plant container for the Non-Yew gardener is the hanging basket. This humble object has become a veritable industry – probably now bigger than the home-owned car industry. Hanging baskets are made of every material and shape with all sorts of clever improvements. Some can be raised and lowered to allow easy watering and re-planting. Others have bowls inside to reduce the need for watering. There are little funnels you can put into the soil so that the water stays there and gradually seeps in, instead of running off. And there are specially formulated long-term fertilisers for hanging baskets made by the best brains in the chemical industry.

Hanging baskets come from an ancient tradition. They might even be derived from one of the seven wonders of the ancient world: the Hanging Gardens of Babylon. They can be seen in Romanian train stations or Greek villages looking simple and charming even to the sceptical Yew gardener. But in Britain, the hanging basket has been adopted by the Non-Yew gardener with such enthusiasm and planted with such riotous mixtures of bright colours, that the socially superior gardener does not dare have anything to do with them.

PAINT

Paint, as Rosemary Verey would say, is 'important'. (Mrs Verey says lots of things are 'important'. Pots are 'important'. Seats are 'so important'. I have no doubt that paint is 'important' too. What I think she means is that if you get these things wrong, your reputation goes in the shredder.)

The first thing about paint is to use the right colour. The second thing is to use the right manufacturer.

In the garden, paint is most frequently used for painting iron or mock-iron furniture. Sometimes it is also used for gates. The colour for these is very difficult. Fashions for Yew gardeners have changed over the years. First there was black. But it was boring. Then there was white. But it was glaring. Then there was dark green. But that became boring too. So then, at last, there was blue. It did not glare and it was not boring.

Other colours have been tried. Prince Charles has painted sea green all over the place, which is a little too distracting. In his earnest search for the right colour, the Prince has even tried baby-bow pink. It does not work, but you have got to give him high marks for trying.

So blue it is. But which blue? Rosemary Verey herself has addressed her aesthetic senses to the problem with her usual thoroughness. Mixing up paint colours herself (very Yew indeed) she has created a blue that is somewhere between navy blue and royal blue. And yet it is not merely blue. It is blue with a dash of something to make it interesting. The extra ingredient rewards attention without being distracting. I think it might be a *soupçon* of purple. So there it is: Verey blue.

'Verey Blue' would sell by the bucket-load to anxious Yew gardeners

One of the fashionable paint manufacturers should rush out to Gloucestershire and beg Mrs Verey for a licence to make her colour. 'Verey Blue' would sell by the bucket-load to anxious Yew gardeners who are not quite sure they have got their home-made blue quite right.

Which brings us to the 'important' question of paint manufacturers. *Gardens Illustrated* once asked an assortment of fashionable designer-types to take on the vexed problem of designing an acceptable garden hut. Only one out of thirteen chose Dulux. Not a single one used Crown. These manufacturers obviously had to be avoided. Their paints are the product of years of high-tec research. They are practical and efficient. No, thank you.

Instead, the most commonly chosen paint manufacturer was the specialist company, Farrow and Ball. The designers chose from its National Trust range. These paints are made to 'traditional' recipes. We are led to believe that they have a more muted look and do not appear 'plasticky'. Other specialist manufacturers mentioned were John Oliver, Annie Sloan's Traditional Paint, Sanderson, Paint Magic and Holman.

In all this paint one-upmanship, Susie Manby surely had the best line. Susie was billed as an 'interior and garden designer in Provence and London' ('Provence' adds a certain *je sais quoi* all by itself). She started with 'trade' eggshell (sounds expert) and then bought artist's 'pure pigments' and applied them 'suspended in an emulsion glaze'. This is serious stuff. Her description of the advantages of this method completed the story: 'The beauty of using paint not specifically designed for outdoors is that it will fade and age well'. Age. Artist's pigments. Fading. Ageing. This is true Yew talk.

In contrast, the Non-Yew gardener has nothing to say about paint colours.

White plastic does not need painting.

BARBECUES AND OTHER EMBARRASSMENTS

The Non-Yew gardener comes into his own when it comes to those 'little extras'. His patch is full of them. Pride of place goes to the built-in barbecue. It is wonderfully practical. Everything is ready for use. It also makes a statement. It says, 'This garden is used for having cheery, convivial parties with our coach-loads of friends'.

Nearby there is the very-much-raised bed. Made with yellow-coloured, concrete blocks, this brings up to waist level those bright geraniums which otherwise would be lurking at ground level and hardly visible at all. Please note the so-called 'random' brick which the concrete manufacturer has thoughtfully provided. This especially large block of concrete is supposed to add an air of informality – as if this was a real, country-stone raised bed in which one had used real stones of various sizes which happened to come to hand.

It is a curious thing: faking age with paint finishes is Yew but faking an old wall with concrete 'random' blocks is Non-Yew.

Another Non-Yew fake is the grey, concrete mushroom offered by Agriframes. How appealing, you might think. But it is more than that. It is practical. The top can be removed to reveal a storage place for your emergency front door key. Ingenious. Unless, of course, thieves read Agriframes' catalogues too.

CHAPTER SEVEN

SUPERIOR TECHNIQUES, EQUIPMENT AND CLOTHES

B ritish snobbery is particularly sophisticated when it comes to things like clothes and tools. The devious subtlety would impress a Ming Dynasty diplomat.

The uninitiated might assume that the Yew gardener would mostly wear smart clothes and use expensive equipment. But it is even more Yew to wear manky old clothes and use bashed up old equipment.

The upmarket gardener choses a mixture, usually, of the old, the smart and the practical. It must be a mixture. To choose everything practical would make one a bore, to choose everything smart would make one a cad and to choose everything old would make one a tramp. Only a blend makes one Yew. The balance to be achieved is obvious to the naturally Yew gardener but is as difficult to explain as the rules of cricket. One can be a little bit smart without spoiling the effect. It helps, though, if one can justify this on grounds of practicality. One is allowed superb secateurs, but one needs to balance them with an old spade and practical hose-fittings.

The key to getting it right is to affect a total disregard for smartness with at least one firm anti-smartness statement.

Black gum boots are very good for this purpose. They are not smart at all. Wearing them is the clearest possible demonstration that one has no pretensions. (And although they are cheap, being black means that at least they are not vulgar.)

Alternatively one can make one's statement with a wheelbarrow. The Yew gardener might buy a builder's barrow. One can say, 'I got it from the builder's merchant for £20.'

The cleverness of this approach is the ostensible statement that one is not competing socially at all. One is not attempting to be superior. It is a clever strategem because it makes one's superior garden (and superior many other things too) look all the more impressive. They are particularly impressive because one is apparently not even trying.

Here then, item by item, is an introduction to this highly complex area of garden snobbery:

GARDEN CLOTHES

The mix 'n match of the old, smart and practical starts with the jersey or cardigan. This should be old. There is no point in ruining a perfectly good new one. On the same basis, the trousers should be positively ancient.

The smart ingredients one mixes in vary according to taste. One option often favoured is the quilted jacket. This may be worn as a three-quarter-length jacket (as per Penelope Hobhouse) or as an outer waistcoat (i.e. without the arms). The approved colour is camouflage green although blue is available for the daring. (One manufacturer actually makes a reversible version so that one can adjust one's colour according to one's exact sense of what feels right at any particular moment.)

Another possible smart element is footwear. Smart boots are made by Barbour and Clares-Dickies. But the classic smart Yew boot is made by Hunter. Hunters are three times the price of ordinary black boots. One should perhaps have an excuse handy for this expenditure. One might say, 'I wouldn't have bought these fancy boots, but in this clay soil they are the only ones with enough grip.'

The colour of one's Hunter or Barbour boots is normally green but, for those wanting to make a bigger splash, blue is available.

The trouble is, blue boots are dangerously close to looking *too* smart. Definitely going too far would be the high fashion gumboots made by DKNY or Le Chameau in France (with leather lining).

Yew theory has it that, if someone looks smart, there are seven things wrong with him:

1,2,3 and 4: he is vain, untrustworthy, self-centred and did not have the sharp edges knocked off him at public school.

5: he must be a *nouveau riche* not to know this.

6: he cannot possibly be a good gardener if he is concentrating so hard on his appearance, as proved by the fact that. . .

7: all the best gardeners follow the dress-down-at-heel code.

To put it another way: dressing smartly for gardening is like owning a Range Rover while living in London. It is the wrong pretension in the wrong place. It breaks the upper-class rule that all pretension must at least make some effort not to appear to be pretension.

One important word of advice on hair styling:

no

YEW CLOTHING FOR INDOORS

Three of the most prestigious gardeners in Britain once gave lectures on the same day at the Chelsea Physic Garden: Rosemary Verey, Penelope Hobhouse and Christopher Lloyd. It was a day of learned discourse but also a day for an authoritative display of Yew clothing style.

Rosemary Verey modelled horn-rimmed spectacles, a cardigan, floral blouse, pleated skirt and – those hits of the season – flat shoes. As she demonstrated, the must-have colours are muddy green, muddy brown and muddy grey.

Jewellery? Yes. It has come back. Rosemary was wearing four lines of small (and therefore real) pearls and a tiny brooch – probably an heirloom.

Her hair was worn white, white, white. Quite shameless. And her hair was styled with curls.

Penelope Hobhouse was worryingly smart with her long mid-green jacket and trousers. Otherwise she did not deviate from the rules: a cardigan and unabashed, undyed hair. Low-heeled shoes, a muddy beige blouse and no make-up completed her alluring 'gardener-come-through-a-bush' look.

What about the gentlemen? There was dear 'Christo' Lloyd wearing his trademark 'pre-war' brown shoes. He was wearing these with a grey suit. He, too, was wearing a cardigan in mud green. That makes three out of three wearing cardigans – these are what the Yew gardener absolutely must wear or else risk being considered badly dressed.

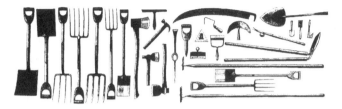

GARDEN TOOLS

The classic Yew garden tool is an old spade which one has had for years. It is made of wood and looks battered. Ideally, one inherited it. A Penelope Hobhouse book shows that she has a veritable museum collection of old wood-shafted spades.

If, sadly, one has not inherited such spades as heirlooms, the Chelsea Gardener garden centre is, as ever, willing to offer instant age and tradition. It has a range of worn old tools at spanking new prices.

An old spade or fork is not compulsory. Practicality and smartness have made the modern stainless steel spade thoroughly acceptable, especially when combined with a traditional wooden shaft.

Among secateurs, one name stands alone: Felco. This Swiss manufacturer makes a range of secateurs the prices of which run from the expensive to the daunting. One justifies the luxury of them by saying how useful it is to be able to send off for replacement parts. Practicality is excellent for justifying one's self-indulgences.

To make up for this show of money, however, the wheelbarrow could be a mangled old metal one of no distinction at all. For those obliged to obtain a wheelbarrow new, the key thing is to make it as basic as possible (without, of course, going so far as to use plastic).

The superior gardening magazine *Gardens Illustrated* once did a survey of wheelbarrows and chose as best the 'Groundsman' by Haemmerlin. The great thing about this barrow was that it was expensive and high quality but kept terribly quiet about it. The pan was galvanised and the wheel at the front rubber. The handles were discreet black. It did not boast but it was shot through with sound design and substantial materials.

Similarly, the best hose for the Yew gardener, according to the same magazine, was a rubber one made by Claber. An interestingly obscure origin and the colour was serious black – albeit with an orange stripe. It looked nothing special yet was decidedly superior. Ideal.

The fittings for one's hose – no detail is too small – would, in a perfect world, be made of brass. Unfortunately most fittings – and in truth, most of the best fittings – are made of brightly coloured plastic. In the *Gardens Illustrated* coverage of this issue, one could feel the staff struggling to chose between the smartness of 'real metal' and the preferred performance of various plastic fittings. They cooed over the looks of a brass spray nozzle made by C.K. Tools then had to admit it was 'top heavy and tiring to use'.

The same kind of mental tussle took place over plastic sprinklers. The report was littered with phrases such as 'ugly colour', 'well-made but loud' and 'hideous colour'.

Then there is the question of where to put the hose when it is not in use. The sight of a green plastic canister at the side of a house is disastrous. There is no easy answer to this problem. One probably needs a hedge, a

'One probably needs a hedge'

GARDEN TOOL FETISHISM.

It is not for everybody, but some Yew gardeners are tool fetishists. Gertrude Jekyll certainly was.

She loved objects made by hand and took the typical Yew gardener's delight in all the ruddy, manual things that are generally done by someone else.

She wrote of the 'lovable quality' of implements and devoted page after page to tools – carpentry and building tools, too.

'Axes and hand-bills are ground, fag-hooks sharpened, picks and mattocks sent to the smithy to be drawn out, the big cross-cut saw fresh sharpened and set, the hand-saws and frame-saws got ready.'

She went on (and on):
'The rings of the bittle are tightened and wedged up, so that its heavy head may not split when the mighty blows, flung into the tool with a man's full strength, fall on the heads of the great iron wedges.'

There is much more where this came from. The woman adored tools with a passion that others reserve for toy trains. And she was not alone. She once met a builder called Clarence Greenfield who was dying of consumption. She took a photograph of him as a keepsake because he was the sort of man who – when he thought of his tools – could not 'bear to go'. That is tool-love for you. Miss Jekyll designed some tools herself and had them made up by a local blacksmith.

The love of tools lives on. The ideal is the

Jekyll adored tools with a passion that others reserve for toy trains

tool made as it was in Jekyll's day – hand-forged by a blacksmith. There is something utterly gorgeous about the heavy, battered, blackened metal that tool-addicts cannot resist.

It does not end with spades, either. Some of the more obscure tools mentioned by Jekyll can still be obtained. The mattock is an axe on one side of the head and a blade at ninety degrees to the person wielding the tool on the other. It is used for 'grubbing out' (wonderful country phrase).

Another traditional instrument is the bill or bill-hook. It is a chopper with a short, thick handle and a blade about a foot long, curving in at the end. It can be used for cutting through undergrowth or – as in France – for pollarding trees. There used to be different designs in every county in Britain. Now there is probably only one blacksmith hand-forging them at all.

Not many blacksmiths still make garden tools. But there is still Chieftain Forge in Scotland. The company makes powerful, hand-forged forestry spades. These are much stronger than one would need for gardening – and the wrong shape, too. The chaps there cannot understand why soft-skinned fetishists from the South contact them despite having no woodland whatsoever. A chap from Guildford kept on ringing Chieftain Forge asking for all sorts of tools – most of which he probably did not use at all. Presumably he just hung them on a wall and occasionally (gulp) touched them.

fence or even a wall to hide such nastiness. Rosemary Verey has a wall. Stone, of course.

What, then, of Non-Yew equipment? It is practical and cheerful – even jokey. The use of plastic is as uninhibited as a streaker at a cricket match. The Non-Yew gardener has a special weakness for gadgets. Among the wizard wheezes he finds hard to resist are 'aerator sandals'.

These are attached to the soles of one's shoes. The spikes underneath are supposed to aerate the lawn as one walks over it. The author knows of one person who, in attempting to use these, became stuck in the lawn and then, being unable to move backwards or forwards, struggled a bit and then fell over, causing his friends who were watching to laugh with so much vigour that it hurt.

A particularly widespread jokey fitting is the brass tap with a handle cast in the shape of a bird, a frog, a duck or a badger. These have been pre-patinated to makes them look old.

The Non-Yew gardener has all sorts of little extra useful things he did not know he needed until he saw them in one of those catalogues that fall out of Sunday colour supplements. One such is the 'Tool bucket and seat all in one'. Tools go into the plastic bucket or the surrounding little pockets. An air-cushioned lid can be put on top of the bucket to provide an instant seat.

Another product that sounds a clever idea (i.e. more trouble than it is worth) is a 'lightweight portable scoot'. It is a plastic seat on wheels. No doubt the next development will be a motorised version.

FERTILISERS, COMPOST ETC.

One of the few things that genuinely cuts across the class system is organic gardening. There are some differences in emphasis, however.

Yew gardeners are especially keen on muck (it is that countryman fantasy again). They like to feel they are close to real, down-to-earth farming-type things.

Similarly, when it comes to massive, enthusiastic, over-the-top use of chemicals, no one can outdo the Non-Yew gardener. He wants thousands of flowers and is willing to use anything Fisons or Zeneca can offer to get them.

He starts off with some Chempak BTD (Base and Top Dressing). Or perhaps Growmore. Then he sprays with a foliar feed throughout the growing season. If he wants to boost his vegetables, he might also throw in some multi-action calcium. When growing 'gross' feeders like chrysanthemums or dahlias, he might also throw in some extra nitrogen. Deluged with a cocktail of such boosters, the plant erupts out of the ground like a NASA space rocket.

ESSENTIAL EQUIPMENT

YEW	NON-YEW
1. Old wooden spade	1. Lawn aerator sandles
2. Battered old wheelbarrow	2. Tool-bucket and seat 'all-in-one'
3. 'Felco' secateurs	3. Brass tap with handle the shape of a bird
4. Mattock	4. Wilkinson Sword 'cultivation set' (tools with twist-off handles)
5. Billhook (hand forged)	5. Hose guides

OF GARDEN BONDAGE

The Yew way to tie up or support plants is to do it with natural materials. String is Yew. Coppiced branches of hazel are Yew. The fact that string rots and it is hard to find coppiced branches of hazel is just hard lines.

Some Yew gardeners would love to use plastic-covered wire and mass produced 'Link stakes' for holding up floppy plants. But this is not allowed. Such practical accessories are strictly reserved for Non-Yew gardeners.

TYING UP PLANTS THE YEW WAY

1. Young branches of hazel
2. Raffia
3. Jute
4. Bamboo canes
5. Willow gates

TYING UP PLANTS THE NON-YEW WAY

1. Wire covered in green plastic.
2. 'Link stakes'
3. Plastic ties
4. Plastic ties which can be glued to the wall
5. 'Y-stakes'

WEEDS

Weeding by hand is very Yew. It shows one is not afraid to have contact with the earth and do the dirty work. Alternatively, the upmarket gardener who does not enjoy getting on to his hands and knees resorts to mulching with bark. It is expensive without being ostentatious.

The Non-Yew gardener has no patience with all this. He blasts the little blighters with chemicals.

LIGHTING

The seriously Yew gardener is not interested in lighting since plants cannot properly be appreciated at night time. The more frivolous decorator sort of Yew gardeners have lighting which is as subtle as possible – preferably invisible. The sources of light are hidden in the ground and in foliage.

The Non-Yew gardener has more fun. His multi-coloured spot-lights shining up out of the fountain are a particularly spectacular feature. This, combined with fairy lights, makes a Non-Yew night-time garden party something you can't forget – however hard you try.

KILLING SNAILS

Both Yew and Non-Yew gardeners use all sorts of methods to kill snails. But the Yew gardener likes to think of himself as a countryman. Therefore he likes to kill his snails in a rugged, Land Roverish sort of way – by stepping on them.

CHAPTER EIGHT
FOLIES DE GRANDEUR

Follies and fun used to be a major part of superior gardens. But nowadays the modern Yew garden is fearfully sober and tasteful. If one wants fun and games one must turn, instead, to the Non-Yew garden.

Animal sculptures – naturalistic or otherwise – are favourite amusements in Non-Yew gardens. Take the 'lawn crocodile'. It consists of three separate pieces of cast concrete which look, when set in a row, as if they are part of a crocodile that is semi-submerged in the lawn. Or how about 'plant pets'? These are colourfully hand-painted birds and frogs with electronic devices that make them chirp or croak when the plants need watering.

Then there are 'cow pat pets'. They are made of cow dung that has been cast into the shapes of a toad, a rabbit and a turtle. One is supposed to place them among the plants where they amuse visitors while simultaneously bio-degrading and feeding the soil.

Another little joke is the miniature cricket team which includes some members whose faces remind one of the Conservative Party front bench. Hedgehogs drive cars and frogs lounge in rowing-boats. Nor let us forget piglets in their many shapes and sizes. The Landscape Ornament Company, for example, offers them sniffing, rootling or sitting. They are made of a resin-bonded, cast stone. Or else one can buy 11½-inch fairies made of 'artstone' with 'fine brass' wings from Geoff Tiney in Market Harborough. In his advertisement for mail order he says, 'allow 28 days for me to catch them'.

The Yew gardener is muttering, how vulgar all this is and how loud and unnatural the materials. That is as may be. But there is far more jollity in a Non-Yew garden than in a superior one.

The only follies and oddities in posh gardens these days are old ones. Towers, Gothic summerhouses and statues of naked women are all acceptable only if they have been blessed by the passage of time. Only if they were created and paid for by people who are thoroughly, long-gone dead are they tolerated.

The high-points of the year for the purchase of such objects are the May and September sale of statuary and garden ornaments at Sotheby's Billingshurst each year. Other auctions are offered by Christie's, Phillips and Bonham's. And there are some specialist dealers.

One may buy – at suitably great expense – terracotta finials from the eighteenth century depicting scenes from Aesop's *Fables*, or a lead fountain base held up by four dolphins, or a Rosso Verona wellhead depicting sphinxes or a bronze figure of Pan playing his pipes.

These are exotic and bizarre images carved out of real stone, marble or granite or else cast in real lead, bronze or iron. It is rather sad that these extravagant ideas have to be ancient to be acceptable.

Yew gardeners are so cautious about newly made features that by far the most usual is the pergola. Sir Edwin Lutyens – Gertrude Jekyll's collaborator and a leading architect – used them. His one at Great Dixter has pillars made of terracotta tiles. But one cannot help thinking that pergolas are only selected by the upper classes because they are so utterly safe. They involve no representations of animals, humans, mythical creatures or anything else. They are mildly formal and made of natural materials.

A few pieces of modern sculpture are found occasionally. But they tend to be of safe subjects: naturalistic representations of animals and semi-abstracts such as the reclining figures of Henry Moore.

Upmarket gardens have not always been so sedate. There was a time when they were made for entertainment. From the Renaissance to the nineteenth century, many aristocratic and royal gardens were places of extravagant display, drama, fireworks and many other excitements.

Italian aristocrats loved fountains and soaking their guests. At Pratolino there was a grotto with many niches and rooms. By a single movement, the host could fill the grotto with water, driving his unfortunate guests to run up the castle stairs. But as they did so, jets of water would spout from every other step, utterly drenching them by the time they got out.

Hidden behind the formal avenues of the garden at Versailles were

**Pergolas are only selected by the upper classes
because they are so utterly safe**

bosquets – areas surrounded by woodland in which all sorts of fantasies were played out. The *Bosquet des Rocailles* – so-called because of the thousands of shells specially imported from Madagascar – was hollowed out to make a large amphitheatre with cascades of water tumbling down from tier to tier. Gilded, small ornamental tables (*gueridons)* were provided on which candles could illuminate the night-time festivities.

Further down was another *bosquet* called the Colonnade in which the centrepiece was a massive marble group depicting the rape of Proserpine. Under the guise of depicting classical scenes, the garden had hundreds of barely dressed or positively undressed young women – politically incorrect

The Grove on the Marsh (now destroyed) and the Grand Canal (now without ship) at Versailles

now, but utterly human and full of life. Louis XIV employed seventy sculptors to create them.

In the *Jardin des Sources* – destroyed in 1776 – some fifty springs of water became little rivulets of less than a foot across. One could step across them to lawns in the middle where tables and chairs were placed when required. It must have been a magical place for a picnic.

The ultimate folly at Versailles was the *Hameau*. Built for Marie Antoinette, it offered relief from the formality of the rest of the place. It was, and remains, a fantasy rustic village. A stream wanders down to a large pond. The half-timbered buildings have thatched roofs – some of them with grass growing in them. There is a mill and some stables. The little box-edged vegetable patch is as charming as can be.

Some regard the *Hameau* as affected, if not an affront – bearing in mind the poverty of the peasantry at that time. But at least it shows that it is possible to be upper class and still have fun. Marie Antoinette would have loved the hedgehog driving a car. If she were alive today, she would probably take the idea further – using a full-size antique car with a huge hedgehog driving. She might create a whole *bosquet* of enlarged animals driving cars around a country lane and filling up at a 1950's garage. Unfortunately, modern Yew gardeners are scared to death of this sort of folly. They fear the social equivalent of Marie-Antoinette's eventual fate – death by guillotine.

IS HADDONSTONE YEW?

Haddonstone, Chilstone, and Minster are companies which make objects that *look* like stone. But these objects – seats, pots, urns, statues and so on – are really made of re-constituted stone. That is to say, stone particles are the major part of a mixture poured into the mould to make them.

Yew

But is 'fine cast stone' Yew?

It is certainly tempting for the Yew gardener. These companies know which buttons to press. They do everything they can to make gardeners think, believe or at least hope that their products are Yew. They show their paving being laid on the terraces of grand houses. They explain that a statue is a precise

Non-Yew

replica of an eighteenth-century one at such-and-such a noble house. An advertisement by Haddonstone boasts of 'traditional English quality' and 'classic designs'. The catalogue even costs money.

The trouble is, the eighteenth-century urn you buy from Haddonstone is not the real thing. They know it. You know it. We can't get away from it.

It is Non-Yew.

GNOMES – SOCIAL OUTCASTS OF OUR TIME

It hardly needs saying that gnomes are very Non-Yew. They are more than that. They are the epitome of Non-Yewness, the unbeatable absolute of the thing – icons in their own time.

They are so repugnant to Yew sensibilities that they are actually banned from the Chelsea Flower Show. The Royal Horticultural Society occasionally tries to pretend that gnomes are banned for practical, non-discriminatory reasons. The shows director Stephen Bennett once claimed, 'The reason [they are banned] is simple – space at the show is at a premium.' This excuse might have carried conviction had he not – in the very same article – also said that ten years previously there were 'gaps all over the place' at Chelsea. Gnomes were banned then, too. They have been banned whether there have been gaps or not. Space is not the issue.

A second excuse was that, at Chelsea, the RHS likes to show garden sundries which people might not be able to find in their local shops. This is another ridiculous cover-up. If non-availability was really a guiding principle, the show would not have (as it does) garden benches which one can buy in John Lewis Partnership stores, let alone stalls promoting gardening magazines which one can buy at one's local W.H.Smith or stalls offering gardening tools widely available in garden centres.

If one persists hard enough in one's questioning, one eventually gets to the truth: Article 15 forbids 'highly coloured figures, gnomes, fairies or any similar creatures, actual or mythical, for use as garden ornaments'. Gnomes, specifically and by name, are banned. It is as personal as that. Breaking down under my merciless questioning, an RHS official finally blurted out 'All right. We just don't like gnomes. We are snobs, so there!'

Other revelations of true Yew attitudes then came tumbling out. 'It would be a bit tabloid, wouldn't it?' and 'You might as well say we could allow in day-glo signs and price tickets on the plants. We don't want it to look like Woolworths!'

Anyway, it is clear that gnomes are currently as far down the social scale of gardening as it is possible to descend. It would be as difficult to imagine Penelope Hobhouse with a gnome in her garden as to imagine her on holiday on the Costa Brava wearing a 'Kiss me quick' hat while sipping a Dubonnet and lemonade cocktail decorated with one of those little brightly coloured umbrellas.

But it was not always thus. Dr Brent Elliott, the chief librarian of the Lindley Library, has revealed in a learned essay that there was a time – before their fall from grace – when gnomes were accepted in upper-class society. They were introduced in Britain by one Sir Charles Isham in about 1867. He had an extensive rockery at his home, Lamport Hall, which he had created twenty years before. He put in some miniature porcelain figures which he bought from Germany. Rockeries were a familiar thing in aristocratic gardens of the nineteenth century and, if one is determined to have gnomes, a rockery seems a good place to put them. Sir Frank Crisp

of Friar Park had over 100 gnomes in his 'subterranean passages and gardens' in 1906. They were probably marvellous.

The word 'gnome' is – unfortunately – a bit of a mistake. The trouble probably arose because of the German phrase *gnomen-figuren* which appeared on the catalogues from which rich British gardeners made their orders. But *gnomen* does not mean 'gnome' it only means 'miniature'.

The short tubby figures which we are familiar with these days are not really gnomes at all. They are dwarfs – as in Snow White and the Seven Dwarfs.

Dwarfs had already come into and gone out of upper-class fashion in the course of the eighteenth century. A character in a poem by Goethe at the end of the century looked back at how people used to admire his garden:

'Every traveller stood and gaz'd thro' the rose-coloured railings

At the figures of stone and the colour'd dwarfs I had placed there.'

But now, many years later, he laments, 'Who would condescend to look at it [his garden]?'[*]

This is a classic case of how there is nothing new under the sun. Dwarfs, gnomes . . . whatever you want to call them, they seem doomed to be objects of aristocratic desire one minute and utterly reviled the next.

In the history of gardening taste we seem to veer between a love of fantasy, myth and imagination on the one hand and a love of clipped restraint, symmetry and control on the other. For the time being, the British upper classes are overdosing on restraint so they have given up gnomes. But Non-Yew gardeners have not. They buy gnomes in tens of thousands every year. Most of them still come from Germany (in the land of Wagner, wild

[*]Translation by Martin Teesdale, 1875.

imaginings are never far from the surface). But there is also a cottage industry of gnome manufacturers in Devon and Cornwall with touching names such as 'Gnome World' and 'The Gnome Reserve'.

The classic modern gnome has a white beard and a bright red pointed floppy hat, and he is smiling. He is so benign and serene, he is surely western culture's nearest equivalent to a Buddha figure. The main difference – appropriately – is that the gnome is always doing something. Buddha can cross his legs and do nothing but meditate. But this would drive a gnome mad with frustration. Only as long as he is fishing (his favourite activity), playing the accordeon or sitting on a potty is he, like his proud owner, in nirvana.

Will Chelsea's harsh ban on gnomes ever be lifted? Will gnomes ever get equal rights with snails and cats (which do appear at Chelsea)? It is not impossible. But gnomes will have to organise themselves. As anyone knows, to get things changed, one needs to create a lobby group. The gnome lobby could be called 'GRUMP' ('Gnomes Resist Unfair Mass Persecution'). Once formed into a lobby they would have no problem getting on to the Today programme on Radio 4. If this woodland path is pursued, it will surely lead to success in the end.

CHAPTER NINE
GARDENING GURUS

As interest in gardening booms, the need for gurus to lead the way has never been greater. As already mentioned, two women have become the leaders of upmarket taste – the arbiters of the acceptable. They are Penelope Hobhouse and Rosemary Verey. These two ladies – in their gardening styles and writings – are the pre-eminent gurus of modern Yew gardening. They produce sumptuously illustrated books which sell in indecently large numbers in Britain and the rest of the world.

For, strange as it may seem, the Yew style is now popular internationally. Penelope Hobhouse has had commissions to design gardens in the United States, Italy, France and elsewhere. These two British women of pensionable age are international superstars – met at foreign airports with chauffeur-driven limousines. It is hard to think of other fields in which anything quite like it has ever happened. In gardening, like nowhere else, it seems more likely you will be a star if you are an upper-class woman of more than a certain age.

Penelope Hobhouse is the intellectual's Yew gardener. Thoughtful and analytical, she is steeped in the history and geography of plants. Name a shrub and she instantly thinks of where it came from and when. This is a very handy way to remember what conditions a plant will probably like. Her designs stress formality yet her greatest strength is making harmonious flower borders.

Rosemary Verey must be considered the ultimate Yew gardener of our time – Gertrude Jekyll's representative on earth. She is similar to the great Gertrude in several ways. An upper-class lady of some physical frailty, she has

Gertrude Jekyll: real, unexpurgated Yewness

HOW TO BECOME A GARDEN GURU
∽ THE COMPLETE GUIDE ∽

There are several ways of becoming a Yew garden guru. One is to spend years studying horticulture, work as a professional gardener and, over time, laboriously turn oneself into a genuine expert while managing to stay young enough to look good on TV. It might work, but there is a much easier method:

1. Marry a wealthy man.
2. Move him to a country house.

3. Read a bit about gardening (here is an extra tip: concentrate on the earliest writers or else on foreign gardens).
4. Create a garden, mixing the formal with the informal.
5. Add a few slightly unusual features.
6. Write a book about it.

This method might fail. But if it does, it will be a first.

First, marry a wealthy man

strong views which she has difficulty in toning down for the sake of being polite. She is wedded to the combination of formal and informal. She is also, like Gertrude, much more of a sensual aesthete than is normally considered decent. Mrs Jekyll wrote lyrically of how she loved to hear the rain fall on a roof above her head. Mrs Verey tells her gardener to let the autumn leaves of her acer lie on the ground so she can continue to look at them there.

Like Miss Jekyll, she has combined various elements in a way that suits the upper classes of her time. Miss Jekyll needed updating. She had decreed that one should have separate borders for different seasons. That was all very well when the rich were rich and garden labour was cheap. But it is not feasible now. So Mrs Verey has come up with plans for gardens which can look good throughout the season and even in winter.

The *grandes dames* Verey and Hobhouse are the doyennes of today but, frankly, they do not tell it like it is. For real unexpurgated Yewness, one has to go to the original source: Miss Jekyll herself.

There was no room for misunderstanding with Gertrude. She was openly, unashamedly damning about things she did not like. She was even rude about stupid servants.

Her condemnations of various gardening practices are Yew gardening, red in tooth and claw:

Hybrid annuals:

'There seems to me to be a kind of stupidity in inferring. . .that all annuals are the better for dwarfing.'

Mass bedding out:

'a garish display of the greatest number of crudely contrasting colours.'

Colour:
'Those who know nothing about colour in the more refined sense get no further than to enjoy it only when most crude and garish.'

Horticultural competitions:
'All the glory is accorded to the first-prize bloated monster.'

Her condemnations are thoroughly Victorian. Similarly, she showed true Victorian romance or even sentimentality about the things she thought gardening was all about:

'A garden's main purpose is that it should be a private place of quiet reward for labour and effort – a place of repose to eye and mind.'

Few of Gertrude Jekyll's ideas were wholly original. Her achievement was to find a sensible combination of the ideas around her which would suit the upper classes. She embraced the idea of 'natural' and 'wild' planting but did not reject formality, for which there remains a great appetite.

The other great Yew guru of the past was Russell Page. He brought modernism – that is to say, simplicity of line – to gardening. He is much admired. His book *The Education of a Gardener* is much mentioned. The only trouble is, few of his gardens survived even his own lifetime. They were works of art, certainly. But his customers wanted something more. Something, they perceived, was in short supply. Romance, perhaps? And something else, too, possibly. Ah yes. Flowers.

As for Non-Yew gardening, it does not have gurus as such. It is the gardening of the people. It is not shaped by individuals, it is shaped by what people actually want: flowers, practicality and reasonable cost. Unfortunately,

GERTRUDE JEKYLL TELLS IT LIKE IT IS. . .

'I have seen woody places that were already perfect with their own simple charm. . . made to look lamentably silly by the planting of a nurseryman's mixed lot of exotic conifers.'

'I do not presume to condemn all mixed planting, only stupid and ignorant mixed planting.'

'The most frequent fault, whether in composition or colour, is the attempt to crowd too much into the picture.'

'When one hears the common chatter about 'artistic colours' one receives an unpleasant impression about the education and good taste of the speaker.'

'I expressed the regret I felt that so much individual beauty should be there without an attempt to arrange it for good effect.'

[This comment was made about Wisley.]

'Frequent repetition of white patches catch the eye unpleasantly'

(Could this mean Sissinghurst?)

as soon as professional media gardeners become experts and travel about a bit, they lose touch with these forces.

Geoffrey Smith comes across on 'Gardeners' Question Time' as a no-nonsense man of the soil. He also writes a column for *Garden News* in which he tells us about such things as new gladioli varieties he is trying out. But every now and again we get a glimpse of creeping Yew tendencies. He once wrote that he is put off the rose 'Sexy Rexy' because of its name. That puts his Non-Yew credentials in some doubt.

Alan Titchmarsh surely began as a sound Non-Yew sort but now he goes in for superior practices such as staking plants with real wood instead of plastic-covered wire. How can one trust a man like that?

Coming from the other side of the garden wall, Stephen Lacey is clearly a Yew gardener bravely trying to pretend he is neutral. In one appearance on 'Gardener's World' he made out that he was going to try some of the brashest dahlia hybrids known to mankind. We will believe them when we see them, Stephen.

The only media gardeners who keep to a thoroughgoing Non-Yew style are those who have not been corrupted by fame. One such is the delightful Bernard Ostler who writes a column called 'On the allotment' for *Garden News*. He plants his 'Outdoor Girl' tomatoes, not worrying a jot about the name, only caring about getting the best results. He is often in his potting shed, 'having a brew' and chatting to George and Pete. Heaven knows if it is all true. He might have a mini-Hidcote back home. But it makes a wonderful image.

THE LATEST FASHIONS

Fashions are constantly being offered up to gardeners in TV programmes, articles or at shows such as Chelsea. Like fashions in clothes, they come in two sorts: those that are re-workings of old ideas and those that are ridiculous. Generally, fashions make very little impact on the mainstream. But some have been persistent enough to approach the point of break-through into either Yew or Non-Yew mainstream style:

ARCHITECTURAL PLANTS

Roddy Llewellyn uses a lot of them. He provides them for style types like Sir Terence Conran. Traditional, flowering plants are thrown out and replaced by aggressive, spikey, punk plants. They have long leaves pointed at the end – such as miscanthus. But Yew gardeners are cautious about them. They fear that a lot of these plants together would begin to make the place seem like the home of a South American drugs baron.

MEADOW PLANTING

This takes to an extreme the love of things 'natural'. The seeds of native plants are scattered about and everything is allowed to grow up to a height of three to five feet until being scalped in the latter part of summer. A few 'Yew' gardeners have been seduced. Miriam Rothschild, a great exponent of this style, helped Prince Charles with a bit of meadow planting at Highgrove. But, contrary to expectations, meadow planting is terribly difficult. Two or three species tend to take over. Prince Charles' meadow has dwindled to a relatively small patch. The Non-Yew gardener has nothing to do with such nonsense. He regards meadow plants as weeds.

COTTAGE GARDENING

This is the most mainstream fashion. Chelsea Flower Show in recent years has been full of cottage-style gardens. Perennials and annuals spill over paths, around ponds and up the side of tree houses and other romantic features. Foxgloves are the classic plants to have in them, conjuring up a safe, nostalgic (fictional) past. This style appeals to all sorts but you do not see it in real gardens very often. The style takes too much expertise to create and too much work to prevent it becoming a blowsy mess.

The cottage look as painted by Helen Allingham

FORMALITY

Sir Roy Strong has been conducting a one-man campaign to bring back strict formality. But most people are dimly aware that a Versailles-style garden at 37 Grimsdyke Terrace could look a touch out of place.

DECORATOR GARDENING

This is taking modern interior style into the garden. Fashionable gardeners like Anthony Noel do very un-Jekyll-like things such as painting flower pots with broad stripes of white and blue. It might catch on in the city but certainly not in the country.

GRAVELMANIA

Gravelmaniacs such as Gay Search and John Brookes kill off the lawn entirely and replace it with gravel or shingle interrupted by occasional plants growing through. It especially appeals to people who are really not gardeners at all. The maintenance work is close to zero. But for true horticultural superiority, there must be work to do and difficulties to overcome. There can be no elevation without frustration.

CREVICE PLANTING

This is a variation on the above. Bricks or stones are laid on the ground leaving little crevices which have some grit in them, through which little plants can grow. Prince Charles (something of a fashion-slave if truth be told) has tried this in his 'terrace' garden. The trouble is, grit is not very well behaved and starts straying on to the brick and stone. It all becomes a bit of a mess. The crevices will probably be entirely taken over by *Alchemilla mollis* in the end.

ESSENTIAL BOOKS

MODERN BOOKS TO BE LEFT ON THE COFFEE TABLE OF THE YEW GARDENER

1. *Plants in Garden History* by Penelope Hobhouse

2. *Making of a Garden* by Rosemary Verey.

3. *The Architecture of Western Gardens. A Design History from the Renaissance to the Present Day*, published by the MIT Press, Cambridge, Massachusetts, USA 1991. 75 scholarly essays. 543 pages. (Obscure yet authoritative, it is bound to impress.)

4. The Royal Horticultural Society *Dictionary of Gardening* (there are four volumes, but one on the table should be enough).

5. *Good planting* by Rosemary Verey.

6. *Colour in your Garden* by Penelope Hobhouse.

7. *The Green Tapestry* by Beth Chatto.

8. *The Well-Tempered Garden* by Christopher Lloyd.

9. *The Chinese Garden* by Maggie Keswick.

10. *derek jarman's garden* by Derek Jarman (although this is too 'politically correct' for some tastes).

CLASSIC BOOKS FOR ADVANCED GARDEN SNOBS

(original editions are vastly preferred to reproductions)

1. *Wood and Garden* by Gertrude Jekyll

2. *Home and Garden* by Gertrude Jekyll

3. *The Education of a Gardener* by Russell Page

4. *Colour Schemes for the Flower Garden* by Gertrude Jekyll

5. *In Your Garden* by Vita Sackville-West.

6. *The English Flower Garden* by William Robinson

7. *Italian Villas and their Gardens* by Edith Wharton.

8. *We Made a Garden* by Margery Fish.

9. *My Garden in Spring, My Garden in Summer* and *My Garden in Winter* trilogy by Edward Bowles.

10. *On the Making of Gardens* by Sir George Sitwell.

ANTIQUE GARDENING BOOKS FOR THE SUPER-ADVANCED GARDEN SNOB WITH ADDED PRETENSIONS AND MONEY

1. *Flora Graeca* by John Sibthorp, ten volumes published 1806–1840 (costs over £20,000 if you can find a set).

2. *Herball* by John Gerard 1633 (must be second edition which is bigger and tolerably accurate).

3. *Paradisi in Sole Paradisus Terrestris* 1629 by John Parkinson.

4. *The Country Housewife's Garden*. and *A New Orchard and Garden* 1618 by William Lawson.

5. *Sylva* 1664 by John Evelyn (with celebrated eulogy to holly).

AUTHORS AND PUNDITS

TOP TEN DEMI-GODS OF GARDENING ONE SHOULD KNOW ABOUT

1. Linnaeus (developed the modern system of plant identification)

Linnaeus

2. Clusius (brought flowers into seventeenth-century gardens)
3. The Tradescants (first of the great British plant hunters)
4. Le Nôtre (French designer of Versailles and other gardens)
5. Gertrude Jekyll (outstanding designer of flower gardens)
6. Bramante (influential in creation of Italian Renaissance gardens)
7. Capability Brown (demi-God or demi-devil, turfed over British gardens)
8. Robert Fortune (first plant hunter into China)
9. William Robinson (proselytiser of the 'natural' look)
10. Russell Page (modernist designer).

MODERN YEW GURUS AND WRITERS

1. Rosemary Verey (books)
2. Penelope Hobhouse (books and international designer)
3. Robin Lane-Fox (*Financial Times*)
4. Anna Pavord (The *Independent* and *Gardens Illustrated*)
5. Peter Parker (*Hortus*)
6. Christopher Lloyd (*Country Life*)
7. Lady Mary Keen (*Independent on Sunday*)
8. Sir Roy Strong (various publications).
9. Stephen Lacey (*Daily Telegraph* and *Gardener's World*)
10. Ursula Buchan (*Sunday Telegraph*)

NON-YEW WRITERS AND MEDIA STARS

1. Bernard Ostler (*Garden News*)
2. Geoffrey Smith (*Garden News* and 'Gardener's Question Time')

Bernard Ostler

3. Alan Titchmarsh (everywhere)
4. Gay Search (books and various)
5. Roy Lancaster (all over the world)
6. Stefan Buczacki (many places)
7. Pippa Greenwood (books and various)
8. Adrian Bloom (has own nursery, books and various)
9. Matthew Biggs (Channel 4 'Garden Club' and various)
10. Adam Pasco (editor of *Gardener's World* magazine)

TRENDY

1. Dan Pearson (*Sunday Times* and various)
2. Wolfgang Oehme and James Van Sweden (American designers)
3. Julie Toll (designer)
4. Noël Kingsbury (author and designer)

NAME-DROPPING
or 'Lutyens knew my father. . .'

We all agree that there is nothing more offensive than name-dropping. We hate it in others and resist it in ourselves. And yet we are frail, wanting the comfort of feeling we are endorsed – as it were – by great names.

Some people can't resist mentioning famous gardening names. They somehow get into the conversation that when 'Christo' visited their garden, he thought this and that and how wonderful he thought their *cannas* were. ('Christo' is the nickname, by the way, of the well-known gardener, Christopher Lloyd).

Rosemary Verey hates any kind of snobbery in gardening.

But as it happens Mrs Verey has met and 'been influenced by' the absolute 'A' list of famous gardeners of our time. And if you were going to drop names – which Heaven forfend! – then these would be the tops. Russell Page gave her advice (Russell Page is ideal. He is now dead, so he is not available to anyone who has not already had him). The late Nicholas Ridley helped her over a tricky design problem (you may think he was only a politician but in fact he was a grandson of Lutyens and therefore a kind of famous garden person by family connection).

Nancy Lindsay taught Mrs Verey 'to look at nature' (Nancy Lindsay was a noted plantswoman and great friend of Lawrence Johnston, the creator of Hidcote).

They somehow get into the conversation that 'Christo' visited their garden

Christo – *dear* Christo, he is so brilliant – he told Rosemary to prune the gleditsia severely each spring so that the canopy did not spread too much. David Hicks – married to Lady Pamela Mountbatten as I am sure I don't need to mention – taught Mrs Verey 'the importance of mowing heights'. Oh yes, that is so important. And let us not forget Sir Roy Strong, formerly Director of the Victoria and Albert Museum. His garden picks up the Elizabethan idea that each part of the garden should have a special meaning. This has been an influence on Rosemary too.

The ideal – and this is hard to achieve for the amateur – is for people to know one has been in contact with famous names without ever having to mention it. *La Verey*, for example, is known to have advised Prince Charles on his garden at Highgrove. But she certainly does not go on about it. Sir Roy Strong mentioned it in his book about royal gardens. He mentioned the other well-known designers who worked on Highgrove too, which included himself.

P.S. In Mrs Verey's book, she does not mention being terribly influenced by Alan Titchmarsh or Geoff Smith. Can this be a mistake?

CHAPTER TEN

GARDENS IN BRITAIN

Visiting gardens is like visiting other people's houses: it is an opportunity to steal ideas or scoff at appalling lapses of taste. The supreme Yew garden of Britain, Hidcote Manor, is a living source-book of upmarket ideas for Yew gardeners. It has most of the classic elements of Yew gardening and shows how to do them well. It has two rows of pleached trees, a grand old Cedar of Lebanon, it has a white garden, a wild garden, interesting topiary and masses and masses of yew hedging.

The second-best-known Yew garden is Sissinghurst in Kent. Every year, hundreds of thousands of people flock to this relatively small site. The main car park is full within twenty minutes of opening. The coaches are already belching out fumes and tourists by the score.

The embarrassing difficulty is that Sissinghurst is not a particularly good garden. It is all right and perfectly Yew. But it is not remarkable. It is famous not so much because of its horticulture as because of its creators.

Sir Harold Nicolson was a diplomat at an interesting time in history.

He knew plenty of government ministers and aristocrats. But more important, Vita Sackville-West wrote a column about gardening, was a literary figure and had a lesbian affair with Violet Trefusis. Some people will go to any lengths to make their gardens well known.

The 'White Garden' at Sissinghurst is the best-known single-colour garden in Britain and consequently many assume it was the first white garden. In fact, Vita Sackville-West got the idea from Hidcote.

The garden is also known for being divided into 'rooms'. Again, many think Vita Sackville-West invented that idea too. But the notion has been around for centuries.

In fact, if one forces oneself to be frank, Sissinghurst has got its little faults. It demonstrates what can go wrong with Yew ideas. Whereas, at Hidcote the white garden is in the shade of the cedar, surrounded by lush greenery – making the white flowers a pleasant relief – at Sissinghurst, the white garden is big and open. The white just glares.

One would like to see the work of the patron saint of Yew

TOP TEN GARDENS IN BRITAIN ❋	
Yew	**Non-Yew**
1. Hidcote	1. Waddesdon Manor
2. Sissinghurst	2. Windsor Castle
3. Upton Grey	3. The Pond Garden, Hampton Court
4. Barnsley House	4. Bressingham Gardens
5. Tintinhull	5. Wisley
6. Helmingham Hall	6. Lister Park, Bradford
7. Hatfield House	7. Balmoral
8. Heale Gardens	8. Tropical World, Leeds
9. Iford Manor	9. The Savill Garden
10. Nymans	10. City Centre Gardens, Birmingham

gardening – the gardens made by Gertrude Jekyll. Sadly there are not many one can visit which have not been altered but Upton Grey is an accurate recreation of the garden she made there.

It demonstrates just how liveable a Jekyll garden was. It was meant for people to enjoy. Beyond the formally laid out beds with luscious sweeps of planting, there is a bowling green and then a grass tennis court that need not look like a tennis court at all when not in use.

The other side of the house has a wilderness area of grasses and native plants leading to a pond. Paths cut in the grass lead along a meandering way.

This is the classic ideal of the enjoyable, civilised garden which can be part of the life of weekend parties and games.

The garden at Barnsley House, created and maintained by Rosemary

Upton Grey: Demonstrates how liveable a Jekyll garden was.

Verey herself, shows a different emphasis. This is a serious garden. It is unquestionably, even unremittingly Yew. It has fashionable plants like alliums, it has a parade of large yews cut to an original shape and it has its *potager*.

If you ask Rosemary Verey which gardens in Britain she admires, she will certainly mention Helmingham Hall. 'Such history,' she says and then goes on to praise the owners Lord and Lady Tollemache.

Helmingham Hall has been extended to add on typically Yew features: a herb and a knot garden. But the herbaceous border leading away from the house would not gain the approval of Gertrude Jekyll. The colour contrasts are too violent – to the extent that one wonders whether they were planned at all or whether the owners have Non-Yew tendencies which they can't quite control.

No such lapses are permitted at Hatfield House, another grand place where the Yewness of it all is magnified by history, titles and new, Yew features. Never mind the history of the Cecil family. Far more important is the association with the gardening aristocracy. John Tradescant the Elder was head gardener before going on to become gardener for Charles I.

Since 1972, the gardens have been transformed by the Marchioness of Salisbury. She has laid out a knot garden in which box encloses collections of historic plants from different periods. This and other lurches back towards historical styles might be regarded by some as 'pastiche'. But the lady is a Marchioness, so most people consider it terribly interesting.

Heale Gardens shows how generations of well-bred owners can make a really gilt-edged, through-and-through Yew garden.

One of them was a diplomat in Tokyo at the turn of the last century. On his return he began a Japanese garden out of sight of the house. This garden is utterly 'wrong' in that it is not much like a real Japanese garden. But it is utterly

Iford Manor: an illustration of the pros and cons of bringing Italian gardening to Britain.

'right' in that it is exactly the sort of pretend Japanese garden that educated Britons indulged themselves in when Japanese design was all the rage. One of the contributors to the magic of Heale was the designer Harold Peto. He is a good name to have associated with one's garden. He was major influence in keeping the formal and Italian elements in upmarket garden design.

The garden he is best known for is Iford Manor which was his own garden. It is an illustration of the advantages and drawbacks of bringing Italian gardening to Britain. Most garden guides politely say that the garden works well. That is an exaggeration. It works well in parts but it is also a warning not to go bananas with Italian artefacts.

It is impossible to deny Nymans' qualification for this list. It is bursting with yew hedges, some of which have been cut to form dramatically high castellations. It also has a particularly fine example of that highly sought-after item: a walled kitchen garden. This was built in the eighteenth century, which is good. It was made into a flower garden early this century, reputedly with the advice of either William Robinson or Gertrude Jekyll. Even better. It is a pity the connection is not more definite. Jekyll would have been ideal. But

Heale House: a really gilt-edged, through-and-through Yew garden.

Robinson would be all right. Robinson wrote the important book *The English Flower Garden* advocating 'wild' or 'natural' planting. Penelope Hobhouse considers him even more important in shaping modern gardens than Jekyll.

Penelope Hobhouse herself no longer has a garden to represent her style of gardening. But one can get, as it were, a '*Souvenir de* Hobhouse' by going to Tintinhull. This is the house and small garden which she and her late husband rented from the National Trust. It is the place to see restrained harmony in planting and design. Don't forget to look for vegetables in the vegetable garden. You will find them if you keep at it.

VISITING NON-YEW GARDENS

Most Non-Yew gardens are private. But thankfully some leading characteristics of Non-Yew gardens are generously displayed in certain gardens open to the public.

One stands pre-eminent among Non-Yew gardens. It is the *crème de la crème* of vulgarity, the grand master of garishness: Waddesdon Manor.

Waddesdon was created by Baron Ferdinand de Rothschild at the tail end of the nineteenth century. The house and garden were made in the best of Victorian taste. That means it is despised and loathed by those who have the best of modern taste. What a delight it is to see how the modern upper classes sneer at what their forefathers did.

Waddesdon Manor used up a great many Rothschild pennies. The Baron bought up 2,700 acres of Buckinghamshire on which he built his monstrous Manor. He entered into 'competitive gardening' with enthusiasm. It was said at the time that gentry and aristocrats measured their importance by the number of plants they bedded out each summer. A squire planted 10,000 and a duke 50,000. The brash Baron planted 60,000. He needed fifty-three gardeners to keep the show on the road.

The main, defining feature is the parterre in front of the house which has 'raised ribbon' flower beds. 'Ribbon' refers to the way the beds curve this way and that in the manner of snakes. They are 'raised' because the middle of these beds is literally higher than the edges. This is meant to show off the violent contrasts of colour within each bed as powerfully as possible. The colour onslaught can then be appreciated from ground level as well as above.

This is Non-Yew gardening carried out with an authority and confidence that it is positively awesome.

A great irony of Non-Yew gardening is that it is practised most prominently of all by those who are, in theory, at the pinnacle of the social scale – the royal family. Partly this is because the Queen is not as interested in gardening as she is in racehorses. Therefore the professional gardeners in her employ have been left to their own devices.

The most outstandingly vulgar must be the flower garden at the East Terrace of Windsor Castle. It is outstanding because the kitschness of the Castle itself – a nineteenth-century fantasy superimposed on a genuine castle – enhances the kitschness of the garden.

It was originally intended as a stylish formal garden with pergola walks and statues. But the whole thing got simplified and cut back. Some statues are still there and so are the remains of a formal lay-out. But in the midst of this there are now tapering rectangular beds planted with nothing but roses. Each bed has its own variety – making a bald, brutish block of colour.

The ultimate Non-Yewness is to take a refined, ancient place and blast it with a totally different gardening style – brilliantly colourful but historically

Foggy Bottom: Mr Bloom is not playing the game.

ridiculous. The Pond Garden at Hampton Court is a prime example. The garden was designed to have exotic plants in the reign of William and Mary. But the Victorians then laid the garden out in the style of a Dutch garden with shallow terraces sinking down into the middle where there is a round pound.

The garden has now been adapted to display mass bedding with fierce colours not only next to each other but on top of each other as well. Tall tulips are underplanted with annuals. So it is a seventeenth-century garden in modern, seaside park style. The final flourish – a rude gesture in the face of historical correctness – has been the addition of a contemporary sculpture of a nude.

Another kind of classic Non-Yew garden is the sort produced by 'plantsmen'. Wisley, the main country home of the Royal Horticultural Society, is a demonstration garden. It demonstrates that 'plantsmen' cannot design. Or perhaps it is not so much that they cannot design as that the idea of design has not entered their heads at all.

Kew Gardens are no better. They include some gems but there are no exits or entrances. The Savill Garden similarly has no heart or focal point. It is full of plants. That is about the best you can say about it.

There is one notable plantsman's garden, however, which is at least consistent and therefore – arguably – successful. This is the garden created by Adrian Bloom. Mr Bloom, with his father Alan, is behind Bressingham Gardens – a leading and highly efficient nursery. He is also known for his garden, Foggy Bottom, which features an enormous variety of conifers. There are short ones, tall ones, fat ones, thin ones, yellow ones and blue ones. There are even green ones, too. Mr Bloom breaks the rules of Yew gardening with admirable gusto. The planting is spotty. He packs masses of different things into a single picture. He is constantly seeking extreme contrasts of colour, size and everything else.

Yet another rule is broken by having an all-conifer garden at all. The Yew gardener likes to have plants which are native or at least which look as though they *might* be native.

Mr Bloom is not playing the game. Shamelessly, he has created a garden that is interesting and cheerful all year round. Quite shocking.

❋

CHAPTER ELEVEN

DANGER: FOREIGN GARDENS

Bruitish gardeners who go abroad are in danger. They come back to Blighty and are tempted to try things which looked wonderful in, say, Nepal but which look absurd in Hampshire.

It is the horticultural version of Spanish hat syndrome: the colourful straw hat which looked just the thing at a resort in Spain looks utterly ridiculous back home in one's local high street.

However much we know this danger, we cannot resist the excitement of bringing back something from a foreign land. We like to show our friends how well travelled we are. A foreign feature in the garden is more subtle (and more charitable to our friends) than a two-hour holiday video.

It is remarkably pleasant to explain that the hole in the wall one has made – or whatever it might be – was a notion one got while visiting a celebrated garden in Shanghai ('You don't know it! Oh you must go!')

At the same time, the foreign element must always be treated with care. The danger is that a Vietnamese bridge one places across the pond will not

altogether harmonise with one's mock Tudor house. There is the risk that a suddenly introduced, rather lonely foreign feature will destroy the painfully established good taste of the place. The Chinese pagoda at Kew Gardens is a prime example of such disastrous errors. (The polite way to describe these things it to call them 'follies'.)

Over the years, though, some foreign ideas have succeeded well enough in Britain to be widely accepted. Yew gardeners have been particularly partial to Italian practices such as high evergreen hedges and terracotta pots filled with box trimmed into the shape of balls. They have happily adopted the idea of a long straight path leading to a statue or something.

Harold Peto and Sir Edwin Lutyens (who was Gertrude Jekyll's partner in designing many gardens) were influenced by their visits to Italy. So was another prestigious landscape designer, Sir Geoffrey Jellicoe. Who would not be? Whisper it

The pagoda at Kew

not abroad, but the best Italian gardens tip most British gardens out of the wheelbarrow. It is embarrassing to admit it, but if one visits the Villa D'Este near Rome and then returns to, say, Sissinghurst, one can only be embarrassed by the small scale, pinched imagination and all-round dullness of the British competitor.

The mighty Neptune fountain at Villa D'Este is a spectacular fanfare of a fountain rising high into the air. Behind it is another fountain – the organ fountain – which used to be able to produce genuine music (it probably

The cascade of the Fountain of the Organ, Villa D'Este, Tivoli.

would do still if only it were looked after by the National Trust).

The Italians, in their heyday, brought theatre to gardening. The Isola Bella – a small island in Lake Maggiore – was re-shaped into a kind of pyramid with ten terraces rising steeply from the water to the peak. Each terrace can be walked along and from nearly every part of the garden one can see another. From a high terrace at the back one can see below a tight parterre of box hedging in baroque swirls. From the quartered azalea garden one can lean over a balustrade and see a formal line of orange trees.

Modern British Yew gardeners have not got the money – or, to be brutal, the aesthetic courage – to imitate such features.

They feel on much safer ground copying the French. The French go in for rigid formality. Their most famous garden designer, Le Nôtre, created gardens which were flat or terraced. Hedges and topiary were arranged with geometric precision. It was terrifically boring and, thank goodness, the British Yew gardener has taken some of the formality but softened it with wild planting to make it more interesting.

To be fair to the French (though heaven knows why), their aristocracy would have passed on a few good ideas had they not carelessly provoked the French Revolution and had their heads chopped off. Versailles, above all, was a fabulous garden until the revolution. This (and failure

TOP TEN YEW GARDENS ABROAD

✤

1. Villa D'Este
2. Isola Bella
3. Monet's garden at Giverny
4. Villa Gamberaia (classic Tuscan garden)
5. The Alhambra (Spain)
6. Yu Yuan (China).
7. Filoli (America)
8. Het Loo (restored Dutch garden)
9. Villandry
10. Versailles (despite the decay)

to hand over its management to the National Trust) has meant it is now a pale shadow of what it once was.

The creator – Louis XIV – used all the resources of the state to make it. He saw that his gardeners would take rather a long time to dig a lake a mile long, for example, so he called in the army to help.

The main avenue down leading down to this lake is now cramped and overgrown compared with what it ought to be. But the greatest loss has been the 'room' or theme gardens which were varied and delightful, no-expense-spared fantasies (see *'Folies'* chapter). They are now being restored – painfully slowly.

While waiting, one can visit the greatest success of French gardening: the delightful one made by Monet at Giverny. Yew gardeners go over to see it by the coachload even though they have to put up with non-gardener tourists (such as American teenagers chewing gum, looking at the ground rather than the garden and talking loudly about their mothers' face lifts). The main difficulty for Yew gardeners, though, is trying to work out what it is that makes Giverny so wonderful. They all have their own theories and they go back home to try to re-create the magic. Unfortunately most people try to re-create Giverny without adding any of the more obvious ingredients:

1. A very wide, straight path.

2. Huge iron arches over it.

3. No lawn.

4. A large lake.

5. A large bridge.

6. At least six full-time professional gardeners.

This is Spanish hat syndrome in action. Many visitors go home and buy a pre-fabricated little bridge and – not having a lake to hand – put it over a 'stream' of pebbles. Please be warned that this does not, of itself, re-create Giverny.

In the late nineteenth century, there suddenly came into the familiarity of Continental gardening, the exoticism of Japan. Impressionist painters, furniture makers and china manufacturers all became terribly excited by Japanese design. The Japanese garden at Heale House was created in this period.

Japanese features then were undoubtedly very Yew. Only the rich and educated knew about them and copied them. But now you can buy a Japanese bird scarer – a hollowed bamboo stick which fills with water, then topples over and makes a bang – from hundreds of garden centres through the land. They have therefore become thoroughly Non-Yew. The same goes for Japanese stone lanterns – objects with a kind of oriental roof which turns up at the corners and inside of which a light can be placed.

Thus have the distinguished traditions of Japanese garden design been reduced to providing naff nick nacks for British gardens. It is important that no one should tell the Japanese about this.

An even older tradition of gardening – in China – has been much less exploited by British gardeners. It is therefore still rarefied and upmarket.

Maggie Keswick wrote a book about Chinese gardens in 1978. As a member of the wealthy Keswick family she brought an aristocratic gloss as well as an appealing personality to Chinese gardening. The ideas of Chinese gardening have not been absorbed – at least not consciously. However, the idea that a garden should respect and harmonise with the site and its surroundings is one which is readily accepted by fashionable young designers of today.

the distinguished traditions of Japanese garden design have been reduced to providing naff nick nacks for British gardens

American garden design has been a far bigger influence. America has embraced modern design in gardens far more enthusiastically than Britain. Thomas Church and other designers developed what later was dubbed the 'California style'. They used informal, curving lay-outs, raised planting beds, plenty of paving, some gravel and timber decks. It was bold and modern. Among well-known British designers, John Brookes is closest to this style. But Yew gardeners do not much like it. It does not go with the distinguished old houses they have (or wish they had).

Instead, California style been taken up by Non-Yew gardeners. Not consciously of course. They have not stayed up at night studying the ground plans of Thomas Church. They are not, surely, aware of those contemporary stars of modern design, the American partnership Oehme and Sweden. No.

The alley of the fountains in the Generalife gardens attached to the Alhambra.

Instead they have watched Dallas. Other American TV shows have doubtless had their effect, too, but Dallas was the one in which the central family had a house with a prominent swimming pool and acres of shameless concrete paving on which the family seemed perennially to be eating breakfast (during the breaks when they were not having sex).

The Non-Yew gardener presumably liked the look of this and decided to imitate. Or at least he must have been encouraged to persist with what he was already doing. Why bother keeping up with fusty old British toffs when one can instead leapfrog to modernity, space and bold 'California Style'. This is 'global village culture' Non-Yew style.

Perhaps Californian design is also at the root of the bizarre obsession which Non-Yew gardeners have with kidneys. This shape, or something like it, was used for swimming pools outside wealthy California homes because the new wave of designers thought it echoed the swirling lines of the surrounding hills. California does have swirling lines of hills. Unfortunately back gardens of terraced houses do not.

Spanish hat syndrome strikes again.

CHAPTER 12

WHATEVER NEXT?

The Yew gardener is always trying to break the boundaries of Yew gardening. We all like to think of ourselves as individualists rather than conformists. So Penelope Hobhouse has been trying out a gravel bed. Rosemary Verey goes in for some carefully garish colour mixes. Such experiments will eventually lead to new forms of Yew gardening. The superior garden is always gradually changing.

Over the last half-century (nobody said gardening fashion changed quickly) the rock garden has gone out of fashion. So has the pure rose garden (all those ugly stems). Shrubs have become more widespread since they are less work than perennials and tend to look better in winter. Topiary (especially in the form of a standard) has become very popular – adding formality and all-year interest without taking a lot of work.

But what of the next few decades? What are the Yew trends of the future?

Here are some highly speculative forecasts:

DAHLIAS AND CHRYSANTHEMUMS

They are going to make a comeback. Writers like Robin Lane-Fox are already publishing articles suggesting we should consider them. The next step is for some utterly Yew garden designer to use them a great deal. Of course, the ones used will have to be carefully selected. They will be species ones or else raised by a superior nursery.

KOHLRABI

These cabbages are becoming a cliché. In any case, they can now be seen at Homebase. That is the kiss of death.

SHRUBS

One day someone will breed a shrub which does not look blobby and has lovely flowers.

PEONIES

Peonies have gorgeous flowers but they do not last long. One day someone will breed a long-flowering peony and receive the grateful thanks of the nation.

BEDDING

Mass bedding will remain Non-Yew. But Yew gardeners will try a smart form of bedding out – as practised at the Bagatelle garden in the Bois de Boulogne. All it takes is restraint, formality and the right colours.

SPECIALITY GARDENING

More Yew gardeners will develop specialities such as maple trees or *spiraea*. If it is good enough for the Rothschilds with their rhododendrons, it is good enough for many others.

TORTURE

The trend towards plants with twisted and tortured stems – such as *Corylus avellana* 'Contorta' – will go further. In the long, cold British winter, there is an urgent need for something interesting to look at.

BOX, HOLLY AND ROSE STANDARDS

Another trend with further to go. These standards look smart and do not take much work. They add height, which is desperately needed in most British gardens.

HEDGES

High hedges can look monolithic. A wavy top – like the wavy-topped wall in Yu Yuan garden in Shanghai – is one solution.

TREES

Visits to French gardens will make Yew gardeners realise what can be achieved by training trees. There will be more pleaching and shaping. There will be more avenues and rows.

TREES AGAIN

Yew gardens will also imitate the French idea of gardens consisting of little more than a selection of small, ornamental trees dotted around on rough grass. It looks smart and is easy to maintain.

BENCHES

For decades Yew gardeners have been destroying their backs by sitting on solid hardwood benches that are an ergonomic disaster. For the first time, one manufacturer – called Gloster – has recently produced a range of benches which is actually comfortable. This revolutionary idea will catch on.

CHAIRS

Stainless steel will become a very Yew material for outdoor furniture. It is heavy (unlike aluminium), it won't rust (unlike iron) and it is expensive. It is hard to imagine a better combination. Yew gardeners will justify the cost by calling such furniture 'an investment'. Yew people love 'investments'.

IRON FURNITURE

Edward Bawden benches will become more valuable than Coalbrookdale benches (instead of the other way around). They are elegant and not many were made. True, they are relatively modern, but time will cure that problem.

PLAYTHINGS

An elegant Yew garden can be blown out of the water by just one red and yellow plastic slide. There will be a boom in Yew playthings for children made of natural wood.

PAVED AREAS

At some point, the Yew gardener is going to have to admit that the Non-Yew gardener has been right. He will accept the need for a bigger paved area. People want to sit in their gardens and dine there, too, without sinking into the mud.

PERGOLAS, ARBOURS ETC

Once he has finally managed to sit outside and do it in comfort, the Yew gardener will want more pergolas and arbours to provide shade and reduce the windchill.

SWIMMING POOLS

The country is dotted with outdoor swimming pools used only a few times a year. Gradually everyone will recognise that indoor pools are best for the British climate. These will have large plate-glass doors which can be opened on sunny days.

CONSERVATORIES

Thousands of British conservatories are freezing in winter and baking in summer. Solid, insulated roofs will become the thing.

CLOTHING

Gradually, despite powerful prejudices, the British upper classes will become smarter. One day it will even become Yew to wear blue Barbour boots. (But someone who goes so far as to wear luxury, leather-lined, camel-colour boots made by Le Chameau, the posh French manufacturer, will surely always be considered an unutterable cad).

ACKNOWLEDGEMENTS

My mother introduced me to gardening and – one way or another – introduced me to garden snobbery. She reported comments made by her acquaintances such as: 'She calls herself a gardener yet she does not have a single clematis!' She told me of the barely veiled horror of some of her friends on seeing that her current front garden consists mainly of low, evergreen shrubs – many of them (good heavens!) dwarf conifers.

Paul Dacre cannot avoid my thanks. He was the one who was utterly appalled that I should have planted a hedge of privet. His reaction – entirely framed by horticultural considerations, no doubt – gave me the idea for this book.

Bill Hamilton, my agent, encouraged me to write a synopsis and then sold it with amazing speed. Mind you, he did not have far to go. He sold it to his wife, Kate Parkin, who is a gardener herself and instantly – encouragingly – understood what I was trying to do.

If I am honest, much of my research consisted of delving into the most unbearably snobbish parts of my own mind and fishing out what I found. But I did consult others. Kate Parkin again and – also from Random House – Juliet Annan joined in the spirit of the thing and shared with me their worst prejudices.

I consulted many people in the business of gardening – from a wonderful, though bemused, Scotsman working at Chieftain Forge to an assistant at Green Farm Plants (I provocatively asked for a select, snobbish plant that none of my friends would have. She replied smilingly, 'most people are not so frank about it').

I owe a particular debt of gratitude to one very kind professional: Diana

Ward, a garden designer based in London. She patiently allowed me to question her persistently. She especially helped me with quite a few of the lists, although I hasten to emphasise that the final versions are very much my own and she bears no responsibility for any errors, let alone the sheer presumptuousness of making such lists at all.

I applied for interviews from the ladies whom I consider the doyennes of Yew gardening – Rosemary Verey and Penelope Hobhouse. Both of them were generous enough to grant me audiences. Mrs Verey valiantly went through with our meeting despite having flu. Mrs Hobhouse kindly gave me soup and subsequently took a joke I made about her in an article like an absolute brick. She, too, gave me help with a few of the lists.

I was delighted when Matt – the Daily Telegraph front page cartoonist and cartoonist of the year – agreed to do illustrations for the cover and inside. He is one of the all-time great cartoonists – in the same Premier Division as Bateman, Fougasse, Jak, David Low and Osbert Lancaster. I am honoured to be in the same book as him.

Anthony Whittome has been my main point of contact at Century. He has been a model of patience and encouragement. Thank goodness for that, since I have undoubtedly been a demanding and difficult author – sending long letters asking for changes to this or that. The excellent designer Jerry Goldie has made the book far smarter than it would otherwise have been and has similarly shown remarkable patience.

However their patience has been as nothing compared with that of my wife, Anne who has uncomplainingly endured sleepless nights looking after our infant daughter so that I could have my rest and write the book.

My sincere thanks to all.

SELECTED ADDRESSES AND TELEPHONE NUMBERS

SUPPLIERS OF GARDEN FURNITURE, ORNAMENTS, etc
Agriframes, Charlwood Road, East Grinstead, West Sussex RH19 2HG. Tel: 01342-328644.

Gloster Leisure Furniture, Concorde Road, Patchway, Bristol BS12 5TB. Tel: 0117-931-5335

The Gnome Reserve and Wild Flower Garden, W. Putford, Near Bradworthy, N. Devon, EX22 7XE. Tel: 01409-241435.

Haddonstone, The Forge House, East Haddon, Northampton, Northamptonshire NN6 8DB. Tel: 01604-770711.

SOCIETIES
Henry Doubleday Research Association, Ryton Organic Gardens, Ryton on Dunsmore, Coventry, West Midlands CV8 3LG. Tel: 01203-303517.

The Garden History Society, 5 The Knoll, Hereford, Hereford and Worcester HR1 1RU. Tel: 01432-354479.

The Royal Horticultural Society, P.O. Box 313, 80 Vincent Square, London SW1P 2PE. Tel: 0171-834-4333

The Royal National Rose Society, The Gardens of the Rose, Chiswell Green, St Albans, Hertfordshire AL2 3NR. Tel: 01727-850461.

COLLEGES, LECTURES AND COURSES
Inchbald School of Design, 32 Eccleston Square, London, SW1V 1PB. Tel: 0171-630-9011.

Museum of Garden History, Lambeth Palace Road, London SE1 7LB. (Enquiries: Mrs Janie Wood, 17 The Grove, Teddington, TW11 8AS.)
The English Gardening School, Chelsea Physic Garden, 66 Royal Hospital Road, London. Tel: 0171-352-4347.

GARDENING BOOKS INCLUDING OLD CLASSICS
Mike Park and Ian Smith, 351 Sutton Common Road, Sutton, Surrey SM3 9HZ. Tel: 0181-641-7796.

NURSERIES, SEED SUPPLIERS AND GARDEN CENTRES
Architectural Plants, Cooks Farm, Nuthurst, Near Horsham, West Sussex. Tel: 01403-891772.

Bakker, P.O. Box 111, Spalding, Lincolnshire PE12 6EL. Tel: 01775-711411.

Blackthorn Nursery, Kilmeston, Alresford, Hampshire, SO24 ONL. Tel: 01926-771796. No mail order.

Bressingham Gardens Mail Order, Bressingham, Diss, Norfolk, IP22 2AB. Tel: 01379-687464.

Crûg Farm Plants, Griffith's Crossing, Nr Caernarfon,

Gwynedd LL55 1TU. Tel: 01248-670232. No mail order.

D.T.Brown & Co., Station Road, Poulton-le-Fylde, Lancashire FY6 7HX. Tel: 01253-882371.

David Austin Roses, Bowling Green Lane, Albrighton, Wolverhampton, Shropshire WV7 3HB. Tel: 01902-373931.
Elm House Nursery, FREEPOST, P.O. Box 25, Wisbech, Cambridgeshire PE13 2BR. Tel: 01945-581511.

Green Farm Plants, Bentley, Farnham, Surrey GU10 5JX. Tel: 01420-23202. No mail order.

Goldbrook Plants, Hoxne, Eye, Suffolk IP21 5AN. Tel:668770.

Hadspen Garden and Nursery, Hadspen Garden, Castle Cary, Somerset BA7 7NG. Tel: 01749-813707. No mail order.

Hexham Herbs, Chesters Walled Garden, Chollerford, Hexham, Northumberland NE46 4BQ. Tel: 01434-681483. No mail order.

Highfield Hollies, Highfield Farm, Hatch Lane, Liss, Hampshire GU33 7NH. Tel: 01730-892372. No mail order.

Mr Fothergill's Seeds, Gazeley Road, Kentford, Newmarket, Suffolk CB8 7QB. Tel: 01638-751161.

The Botanic Nursery, Bath Road, Atworth, Nr Melksham, Wiltshire SN12 8NU. Tel: 01225-706597. No mail order.

Thompson and Morgan, London Road, Ipswich, Suffolk, IP2 OBA. Tel: 01473-688821.

Washfield Nursery, Horn's Road (A229), Hawkhurst, Kent TN18 4QU. Tel: 01580-752522. No mail order.

The note 'no mail order' may seem disappointing but many of these nurseries appear at Royal Horticultural shows.

GARDENS
Barnsley House, Barnsley, Cirencester, Gloucestershire. Tel: 01285-740561.

Bressingham Steam Museum and Gardens, Bressingham, Diss, Norfolk. Tel: 01379-687386.

Hampton Court Palace, East Molesey, Surrey. Tel: 0181-781-9500.

Hatfield House, Hatfield, Hertfordshire. Tel: 01707-262823.

Heale Gardens, Middle Woodford, Salisbury, Wiltshire. Tel: 01722-782504.

Helmingham Hall, Stowmarket, Suffolk. Tel: 01473-890363.

Hidcote Manor Garden, Hidcote Bartrim, Chipping Campden, Gloucestershire. Tel: 01386-438333.

Iford Manor, Bradford-on-Avon, Wiltshire. Tel: 01225-863146. Nymans, Handcross, Nr Haywards Heath, West Sussex. Tel: 01444-400321.

Sissinghurst Castle Garden, Sissinghurst, Nr Cranbrook, Kent. Tel: 01580-712850.

Tintinhull House Garden, Tintinhull, Yeovil, Somerset.

Waddesdon Manor, Waddesdon, Nr Aylesbury, Buckinghamshire. Tel: 01296-651282.

Wisley (Royal Horticultural Society's Garden), Woking, Surrey. Tel: 01483-224234.

SUPPLIERS OF GARDENING EQUIPMENT AND CLOTHES
Barbour Footwear, Tweedbank Estate, Galashiels, Selkirkshire TD1 3RS. Tel: 01896-753069.

Burton McCall (sells Felco secateurs), 163 Parker Drive, Leicester, LE4 OJP. Tel: 0116-2340800

Chieftain Forge, Burnside Road, Bathgate, W. Lothian, Scotland EH48 4PU. Tel: 01506-652354.

Haemmerlin, The Washington Centre, Halesowen Road, Netherton, West Midlands DY2 9RE. Tel: 01384-243243

Hunter Wellingtons, The Gates Rubber Company, Edinburgh Road, Dumfries DG1 1QA. Tel: 01387-53111

James Purdey & Sons (sells leather-lined boots by Le Chameau), 57 South Audley Street, London W1Y 6ED. Tel: 0171-499-1801.

Willowdale Products (sells Claber hoses), Unit 3 Station Road Industrial Estate, Winslow, Buckinghamshire MK18 3EQ. Tel: 01296-715652.

MAGAZINES AND NEWSPAPERS
Amateur Gardening 01202-680586.

Garden Design, P.O. Box 5429, Harlan IA 51593-2929, USA. (Editorial offices: 100 Avenue of the Americas, New York, NY 10013, USA.)

Garden News 01733-898100.

Gardens Illustrated 0171-4702400.

Hortus 02544-260001.

Pacific Horticulture, P.O. Box 485, Berkeley, CA 94701, USA.

Your Garden 01202-680603.

INDEX

PICTURE CREDITS

The author and publishers wish to thank the following for permission to reproduce material:

The Royal Horticultural Society Lindley Library (pages 1, 112, 113, 117), *Garden News* (page 15), *Gardens Illustrated* (page 15), the BBC (page 18), Fleur Olby (page 18), The National Trust and Eric Thomas (page 19), Pat Brindley (pages 27, 28, 29, 30, 34, 37, 43, 46, 50, 78, 79), Hulton Getty (pages 44, 45 and 127), Washfield Nursery (page 54), Elm House Nursery (page 54), Sotheby's (page 81), Haddonstone (pages 89 and 111), Felco (page 103), the Bridgeman Art Library/Chris Beetles Ltd., London (page 124), Bernard Ostler (page 128) and Adrian Bloom (page 137). The photographs on pages 4, 56, 58, 59, 60, 84, 85, 131, 133 and 134 are © James Bartholomew.

Matt drew the cartoons. Line drawings were provided by Simon Roulston. Other photographs were taken from *Old London Gardens* by Gladys Taylor, *A Week in Versailles* by Paul Gruyer, *The Formal Garden in England* by Reginald Blomfield and *Garden Ornament* by Gertrude Jekyll and Christopher Hussey.